He's HOT She's HOT

What to Look for in the Opposite Sex

Jeramy & Jerusha Clark

WATERBROOK
PRESS

HE'S H.O.T., SHE'S H.O.T.
PUBLISHED BY WATERBROOK PRESS
2375 Telstar Drive, Suite 160
Colorado Springs, Colorado 80920
A division of Random House, Inc.

Details in some anecdotes and stories have been changed to protect the identities
of the persons involved.

ISBN 1-57856-412-3

Library of Congress Cataloging-in-Publication Data
Clark, Jeramy.
    He's H.O.T., she's H.O.T. : what to look for in the opposite sex / Jeramy and Jerusha Clark.
        p.   cm.
    ISBN 1-57856-412-3
    1. Mate selection. 2. Mate selection—Religious aspects—Christianity. I. Title: He's
HOT, she's HOT. II. Clark, Jerusha. III. Title.

HQ801 .C533 2001
646.7'7—dc21
                                                            00-050974

Printed in the United States of America
2001—First Edition

10 9 8 7 6 5 4 3 2 1

To Louie and Louise Moesta,
whose marriage of fifty years
and legacy of heroic faith inspires and blesses us.
For the countless hours you have invested in us
and for the love you have shared, thank you.
Oh brethren!

Contents

About That Word...

Pepper, Danger, and High Voltage

Hot, you know, can mean a lot. Like "actively conducting an electric current or containing a high voltage," the dictionary says. Or check out this definition: "stolen recently or otherwise illegal and dangerous to possess." Or how about "sharply peppery or pungent"? In fact, our dictionary actually gives a total of thirty different meanings for this little three-letter word.

Of those thirty, the definition closest to what's probably in *your* mind when you say someone's "hot" is this one: "extremely exciting or interesting; sensational." You probably use the word in this way when a person's looks are especially appealing to you, while no doubt the ultimate in hot for you is that has-it-all kind of person— someone you find "sensational" and "exciting" and "interesting" in personality and intellect as well as in appearance.

Our goal for this book is to make this little word even hotter for you. We want to turn hot into H.O.T.—for Holy, Outrageous, and Trustworthy, an acronym we hope you'll never forget. By the time you get to the last page, we trust you'll have both a clear vision of what God esteems in a man or woman, as well as your own practical and biblical strategy for determining what to look for in the opposite sex.

Why This Book?

In more than a decade of combined ministry experience with students and single adults, we've found that their most persistent and perplexing struggles have to do with their relationships with the opposite sex. So a year ago we wrote a best-selling book called *I Gave Dating a Chance.*

If you haven't read it, we'll go ahead and tell you the book's main point: We answer the question "Can dating be an option for young adults who love the Lord and long to please Him?" with a big "Yes!" We explain why we believe single Christians can enjoy godly relationships if they approach dating from God's perspective and according to His guidelines. We also discuss how believers can get to know one another by responding appropriately to romantic feelings. We write about the healthy emotional, physical, and spiritual boundaries that God enables us to maintain when we walk in step with the Holy Spirit. And we explore important issues such as sexual purity and accountability.

God has taught us much more about all this than we were able to include in our book, and we've continued to see how students in our church's youth group need to continue examining principles in this arena. Meanwhile, the end of another school year drew near, and a few parents asked us to contribute to keepsake books they were creating to honor their graduating son or daughter. One of the subjects they asked us to write about was the importance of choosing a godly mate. Other conversations and situations forced us to think about this issue as well. Honestly, we couldn't get away from the topic!

As we organized our thoughts, it became clear that knowing how to choose wisely whom to date and eventually marry was probably the most crucial aspect to healthy relationships with the opposite sex. God has taught both of us the importance of finding a companion of quality and character. And now that we've enjoyed a great start to our own marriage, we can tell you NOTHING beats having a life partner who loves the Lord and who is wild about you, crazy about life, and completely trustworthy.

Start Here

Our ultimate source for the ideas in this book is God's Word—the Bible. You may be a little skeptical about that, particularly when it comes to choosing a person of the opposite sex to date or marry.

"Isn't the Bible outdated on this topic?" you may ask. If you sincerely explore the Scriptures, we think you'll discover it really isn't. We think that in your heart and mind you'll catch a glimpse of what's expressed in a prayer that's thousands of years old: "Your word, O LORD, is eternal.... Your laws endure to this day." (That prayer itself is in the Bible—Psalm 119:89,91.) God's Word is no less useful and reliable for us in the twenty-first century than it was thousands of years ago. It's just as much alive and on-target as ever, and it always will be.

The Lord hasn't changed either, and He never will. He said it Himself: "I the LORD do not change" (Malachi 3:6). So we need not worry that the Bible can't keep up, because we're talking about the living, unchanging words of the eternal, unchanging God.

But then you might have another concern that goes like this: "Won't the Bible tell me that to be godly I have to marry someone I'm not attracted to?"

So many people have this fear! In fact, both of us went through a period of thinking that in order to be righteous we would have to "settle" and marry someone we weren't attracted to, someone whose idea of a good time was reorganizing the closets before Tuesday night bingo.

But both of us found that God had designed a far better "dream person" for us than we ever could have for ourselves. We didn't have to "settle" on any front, because God knew us and had our best in mind.

He has the best in mind for you, too, as He does for all His children. His Word tells us, "The LORD longs to be gracious to you; he rises to show you compassion. For the LORD is a God of justice. Blessed are all who wait for him!" (Isaiah 30:18).

That phrase *longs to be gracious* tells us that God delights to show His children favor, even to the undeserving.

And He "rises to show you compassion." God can feel your deepest needs, and He gets up and gets active in order to be kind toward you!

He's also "a God of justice." He certainly won't hold out on you unfairly. He's not out to deprive you of being with someone fun or engaging. He isn't sitting in heaven calculating how to wreck your life by giving you the most miserable husband, wife, or prom date possible.

So looking to the Bible will never ruin your dreams for an attractive and fun companion. In fact, it may raise your standards even higher!

"But," you may still wonder, "I've never found the words *dating* or *choosing a mate* in my Bible's concordance. The Bible must not have anything to say about those subjects." Those topics don't appear in our concordance either. But 2 Timothy 3:16-17 reminds us that "*all* Scripture is God-breathed and is useful for teaching, rebuking, correcting and training in righteousness, so that the man [or woman] of God may be thoroughly equipped for *every* good work."

You can be guided and coached in *all* areas of righteousness by the Word of God, and that includes being thoroughly equipped to find a godly date and eventually a godly mate. We believe you'll see that God speaks clearly about the core traits Christians should look for in the opposite sex. If you search for and listen to His guidance, He will reveal His plan to you.

If you're skeptical about the Bible on any of these fronts, let the Lord show you how perfect His Word really is. Simply pray this prayer from the Bible: "Open my eyes that I may see wonderful things in your law" (Psalm 119:18).

The Lord used many experiences to point us to what He desired us to look for in a companion. He also used His Word to powerfully convey the truths that we will share with you in the chapters to follow. So we pray that by seeing how He directs us in this critical area of life, you will grow not only in the wisdom of relationships, but also in your appreciation for the practicality and usefulness of God's marvelous truth.

The Road Ahead

In the next eleven chapters, we want to do more than instruct you about what to look for in the opposite sex. We want to go beyond simply outlining how to determine whether someone is H.O.T. according to God's standards. We also want you to examine your own life and determine whether *you* are becoming a H.O.T. man or woman yourself, because a truly H.O.T. guy or girl won't be drawn to you if you aren't also Holy, Outrageous, and Trustworthy. So we'll investigate what a dynamic and growing relationship with Christ looks like. We'll dive into talking the talk and walking the walk of an authentic believer.

Near the end of the book, we'll examine what happens when two H.O.T. people meet. How do they take the next step in building a healthy and godly relationship?

We'll conclude the book with some essential parting words on never settling for anything less than God's very best. As Psalm 37:4 discloses, He wants to fulfill the desires of your heart. Still, you may have to wait some time before it's His will that you meet the right H.O.T. person. We waited a long time, but it was more than worth the wait!

Now…let's get to it!

Making the Choice

Your Final Answer?

You're probably too young to remember, but once upon a time in a galaxy not too far away, a game show called *Let's Make a Deal* thrilled audiences with its spectacular prizes and wacky games.

The contestants came from the studio audience, which kept excitement high both on and off the stage. When chosen, the contestants would play a simple game to win something, and the prizes ranged from cash to appliances, furniture, and electronics—nothing too sensational or expensive. But these prizes became bargaining chips for the second round.

During round two, the player could either leave, satisfied with his new toaster oven or TV, or he could "make a deal" with host Monty Hall. If he chose to deal, the contestant traded his prize for what lay behind one of three huge doors.

Since no contestant had any idea whether the hidden prize would be something better or worse, an element of risk existed. By taking that risk, the player might walk away with a brand-new car or thousands of dollars in cold, hard cash. Then again, the wrong door might reveal a family of monkeys dressed like baseball players, chewing on peanuts and swinging inflatable bats. (No kidding, they really had stuff like that! And get this—you didn't even win the monkeys.) If the contestant later walked away with a car, he would probably feel he'd made the best pick of his life. On the other hand, seeing the baseball-playing monkeys could definitely leave him depressed over his decision-making skills.

Almost all game shows come down to one make-or-break choice. And the stakes have only escalated in the years since *Let's Make a Deal.* Now America sits glassy-eyed as Regis Philbin helps discover who wants to be a millionaire. Contestants aren't risking a new lawn mower anymore. They're playing with six- or seven-digit figures.

If you haven't seen the program, *Who Wants to Be a Millionaire?* is played like this: The contestant must answer fifteen multiple-choice questions to win the million. The first question is worth a measly $100, but eventually the money starts doubling and you can win serious dough.

At each level, the player has the option to take the money he's already won or risk it to go on to the next question. Once his winnings reach $32,000, that much is guaranteed. So if you've won $250,000 and answer the next question incorrectly, you forfeit $218,000. You lose all but the guaranteed $32,000.

Yes, indeed, the game-show stakes have increased exponentially from the *Let's Make a Deal* days. If a player on *Millionaire* chooses wisely, he walks away with a truckload of money. But if he chooses poorly, he winds up losing big time.

In reality, however, the contestant in both these examples loses nothing except the *idea* of winning. After all, you don't play with your own dollars on *Millionaire,* and even the cheapest beginning prizes on *Let's Make a Deal* were never yours to begin with. In the land of game shows, you risk nothing except the *chance* to win something unexpected. Your participation in the game makes a difference, but it won't cause you personal loss.

(Protection from personal loss may be changing though. We saw a brief segment of a British game show in which a nice couple from a London suburb was asked a trivia question in the category of "Geography" to win some prize. Apparently as part of the game, the couple had risked their family car on the question. Unfortunately, they answered incorrectly and then watched as their car was lowered into an industrial crusher. In moments it was turned into a neatly compressed square of metal.)

But most game shows today are not reality. In real life, you make choices every day, all day long, that affect your life, even when you might feel you're "playing" with things that aren't yours or that your choice won't matter *that* much.

Some choices do in fact matter a great deal. Some choices are risky, and making the right decision requires wisdom. If you lie to your parents, you risk getting grounded or, worse, losing their willingness to trust you. If you choose to do drugs, you risk injuring

your body for life. If you have sex before marriage, you risk preg-
nancy, STDs, and psychological trauma. You may even risk facing
these consequences if you "fool around" without going "all the
way." Some choices make the difference between a good life and a
miserable one.

Choosing whom to marry is a life-altering decision that *matters*. Whom you marry makes the difference in almost every area of
life—family, friends, and even your walk with the Lord. Next to
accepting Jesus as your Savior, choosing whom to marry is the
biggest decision you will make.

"Hold on," you say. "I'm nowhere near ready for marriage.
Why do I need to think about this now? I thought this book was
going to help me look for the right people to date."

This book *will* help you make wise choices and date according
to God's standards. But we want you to think about where those
choices eventually lead.

As a young person who desires to honor the Lord, you want to
please Him when you eventually marry. Why not learn now how
to determine whether a person of the opposite sex will complement
you and spur you on in your relationship with Jesus?

Now is the time to start thinking seriously about your standards for a life partner. If you begin to formulate godly ideas about
what you desire in a spouse, you'll be better able to find your prince
or princess without having to kiss a bunch of frogs.

It doesn't work to date willy-nilly and expect that someday
you'll find a man or woman worth marrying. Choose wisely now,

for your choices along the way will influence and shape your final choice. By learning wisdom in the smaller choices now, you prepare yourself for that later life-changing and all-important decision of choosing whom to marry.

"We Rent Wedding Rings"

For making those wise choices, you won't find much help from the world. The world's view of marriage is a poor one. Next time you watch television or go to the movies, count the number of married couples you see who have happy, healthy relationships. Compare that number with how many couples you see who are having affairs, or are always arguing, or whose love for each other has died. Hollywood doesn't usually take marriage very seriously. If you go by what you see on TV and in the movies, you might easily think of marriage as boring, dreadful, or a total joke.

So it's no surprise that the world considers divorce the normal next step when a husband and wife don't see eye to eye. It's "normal" for a person to have one, two, or three ex-spouses. Divorce has been completely integrated and accepted in our society. Divorce proceedings have even become "entertainment," as couples air their dirty marital laundry—the scandals, the betrayals, the pain—before thousands of viewers. Studio executives must think portraying a healthy, happy marriage would be boring by comparison.

The world's easy escape clause of divorce enables people to make the decision to get married with little or no thought. In fact, isn't that what many television and film couples do? Over a few drinks together, they decide to tie the knot. Then they make a quick trip to Vegas to get married. They "go for it," because it feels right at the moment.

It's no wonder that the divorce rate has skyrocketed—to more than 50 percent for those marrying for the first time and to over 75 percent for remarriages. The world views the choice of whom to marry as not much more serious than buying a dress or ordering a dish off a menu: If you don't like it, you can exchange it or send it back. A high-priced jewelry store in a Hollywood neighborhood actually advertised, "We rent wedding rings." Wear the ring for the "trial" period, and if you don't care for the person you married (and chances are you won't), you can turn the ring in until you're ready to try again.

But to be fair, this negativity about marriage isn't simply the creation of the modern media. As far back as 1678, a French moralist said, "There are good marriages, but no delightful ones." Who would want to get married with that kind of recommendation?

Is this how we're to view marriage? Are all marriages doomed to be "good" but never "delightful"? Is marriage just a bad joke?

'Til Death Do Us Part

The world may not take marriage seriously, but God certainly does. He designed marriage as a lifelong commitment between a man and woman. He made clear His intentions for marriage when He Himself matched and married Adam and Eve in the Garden.

He designed marriage as the miracle of "two becoming one." He arranged for spouses to be bonded—physically and emotionally—until death separates them. That's why the marriage vows require a husband and wife to cherish, love, and serve each other "until death do us part." God intended marriage to be a life-changing and lifelong covenant. To the Lord, marriage is a life-and-death matter.

Jesus doesn't mince words when it comes to divorce, as we can see in the following selections from the contemporary translation of the Bible called *The Message*. Several Pharisees are confronting Jesus to test His views. They badger Him:

> "Is it legal for a man to divorce his wife for any reason?"
>
> He answered, "Haven't you read in your Bible that the Creator originally made man and woman for each other, male and female? And because of this, a man leaves father and mother and is firmly bonded to his wife, becoming one flesh—no longer two bodies but one. Because God created this organic union of the two sexes, no one should desecrate his art by cutting them apart." (Matthew 19:3-6)

Jesus boldly declares that divorce destroys God's art. It cuts apart two individuals whom He has firmly bonded together. This separation cannot be done without great pain and suffering to both people. The Lord knows that divorce ravages His design for life and love.

But the Pharisees don't give up.

> They shot back in rebuttal, "If that's so, why did
> Moses give instructions for divorce papers and divorce
> procedures?"
>
> Jesus said, "Moses provided for divorce as a con-
> cession to your hardheartedness, but it is not part of
> God's original plan. I'm holding you to the original
> plan, and holding you liable for adultery if you divorce
> your faithful wife and then marry someone else. I
> make an exception in cases where the spouse has com-
> mitted adultery."
>
> Jesus' disciples objected, "If those are the terms of
> marriage, we're stuck. Why get married?"
>
> But Jesus said, "Not everyone is mature enough to
> live a married life. It requires a certain aptitude and grace.
> Marriage isn't for everyone....But if you're capable of
> growing into the largeness of marriage, do it." (19:7-12)

Notice what Jesus reveals about the seriousness of marriage. First of all, God intended marriage to last a lifetime and allowed divorce only because of the stubborn and unyielding hearts of His people.

Second, Jesus holds us to the original standard, which deems a person guilty of adultery if he or she divorces a faithful spouse and remarries.

And finally, Jesus reveals that marriage is such a big deal that not everyone can or should do it. For some people marriage is too great a commitment, too hard a course. It's fascinating that Jesus' disciples, not the Pharisees, object, "But Lord, that means we're stuck with whomever we choose." Even His most committed followers had a problem with the "forever" part of marriage! And Jesus confirms the truth of their conclusion. Because you're "stuck" once you make the choice, every person should weigh the gravity of marriage before taking the vows.

From the beginning, God planned marriage to be a lifelong commitment. He wanted men and women to take it seriously. And here's the bottom line: "'I hate divorce,' says the LORD God of Israel" (Malachi 2:16). The Lord views marriage so highly that He cannot stand to see it torn apart.

We should have this same mind-set. When it comes to marriage, our Lord makes it clear that once we've taken the vows, once we seal the covenant before Him, He desires and expects us to follow through until death do us part.

Tragically, many Christians have followed the ways of the world and have reneged on their commitments, breaking their covenant vows. Today the divorce rate in America among Christians is equal to that of nonbelievers, and it continues to grow at a frightening rate. Christians seem to believe the lie that if you choose poorly the first time, you can simply get out and start again.

As a young adult who has the chance to make the right choice the first time, take the Lord's words seriously. Regard marriage as He does and plan to make a lifelong commitment when you find a person of godly character. Make the selection process as important to you as it is to Him.

Learn *now* to pick your dates according to the same biblical standards you have for a spouse. When you do, you'll set yourself up for successful relationships. Then you can date and eventually marry a person who is holy, outrageous, and trustworthy.

But Wait—There's More!

You can see the sharp contrast between the world's view of marriage and God's view. Now we'll give you a few more reasons why marriage is such a major life-decision.

These reasons originate in God's purposes for creating marriage. First, God instituted marriage because He found it wasn't good for man to be alone (Genesis 2:18). God wanted man to have a mate who would satisfy part of his need for love and intimacy. Alone, he could not have these needs met. Sharing his life in marriage, however, he could be completed, fulfilled, and delighted.

Because God intended marriage to solve the problems that come from being alone, you need to search for a spouse who will meet your needs for love and intimacy. Look for a mate who can be trusted with your vulnerability. God saw that it was "not good" for man to be alone without a companion, but it's worse for a man or woman to feel alone in marriage. Your choice of a spouse determines whether you will be fulfilled or lonely in marriage.

Another reason the Lord created marriage was to reflect His love for the church. That's why husbands are commanded to love their wives as Christ loved the church, giving Himself up for her (Ephesians 5:25). In *The Mystery of Marriage*, Mike Mason expands this idea: "The love between a husband and wife is a participation in the love of God for the whole human race."

God intended marital love to mirror His love for people in a unique and precious way. Think how serious that makes marriage! If you choose wisely, your marriage can be a powerful testimony of God's gracious love. But if you choose poorly, not only do you miss the privilege of reflecting His love, but you also risk distorting the way others perceive that love.

God also designed marriage for the purpose of completing and complementing His children. It's no surprise that we all have needs ("gaps") that we can't fill on our own. Instead of filling them directly, the Lord sometimes elects to use other people.

When He created Eve for Adam, the Lord made it clear that she was a helper and completer for him (Genesis 2:18). Only together did Adam and Eve make creation "very good" (1:31). The husband-wife relationship is complementary and fulfilling in a way no other relationships can be.

In the film *Rocky*, the tough-as-nails prizefighter meets and falls in love with shy Adrian, who works in a local pet shop. Adrian's brother Paulie, a lowlife character who works in a meat factory and aspires to become a debt collector for Philadelphia loan sharks, can't understand what Rocky sees in his sister.

"I don't get it," he says. "What's the attraction?"

In his husky, muddled speech, Rocky voices, "I dunno. Fills gaps, I guess."

"What gaps?" Paulie questions incredulously.

"She's got gaps. I got gaps. Together we fill gaps."

If you want to find someone whom God can use to "fill gaps" in your life, you need to make careful decisions. The Lord desires and intends to use your spouse to mold and complete you. Wait for a person with whom you can unite to be "very good" in His sight.[1]

Not-So-Perfect Storms

Finally, we want to mention one more reason that marriage is such a huge decision.

Without sin, maybe marriage wouldn't be such a huge decision. Sinless spouses wouldn't argue or hurt each other, so you could probably marry whomever you wanted and be happy. But let's get back to the real world. Since sin perverted God's intentions for marriage, we must face the reality that marriage will be difficult and trying at times. To weather the inevitable storms of marriage, you need to make smart decisions starting with your first date.

And there will be storms. "No one has ever been married," writes Mason, "without being shocked at the enormity of this price and at the monstrous inconvenience of this thing called intimacy which suddenly invades one's life."

Mason likens the trouble to a massive tree, which sprouts and grows in the middle of your house. There's no way to maneuver or live without constant thought and deference to the tree. You must change your patterns and lifestyle to fit with it.

Marriage changes your life, and we both can tell you that sometimes you won't like the changes. You'll even get annoyed at "little things"—your wife likes chocolate more than "real food," or your husband needs every tool on the Sears Craftsman shelf.

What's worse, you'll find yourself arguing over these petty things as if they were life-and-death matters. You'll slam doors or yell or cry over whether he rinsed his dish well enough or whether she bought the right kind of milk.

Marriage doesn't lessen the struggles of life. In fact, in some ways it heightens and highlights them, making them more painful because they're now doubly personal. Two people sharing each other's burdens (or creating burdens for each other) make the heart-aches of life more keen. Robert Louis Stevenson once said that marriage is like life—it's a field of battle and not a bed of roses.

You will face difficulties in your marriage, and one of the best ways we know to mitigate those struggles is to have carefully decided whom you will marry. Hold out for someone with whom you can struggle and grow, not struggle and give up.

Now and Later

Marriage—the wonderful gift which made the "not good" of man's loneliness into a "very good" proposition…the terrific privilege a man and woman have to reflect God's love…the gracious place in which gaps can be filled…and the field of battle in which hearts are strengthened through pain—cannot be entered into lightly.

Choose wisely both now and later. Right now, learn to develop relationships with men and women who resemble someone you would want to marry. Eventually, you may make the life-changing decision to take the vows of marriage. Having trained yourself to recognize godly companions along the way will make your choice of a spouse a more secure one.

Holy Is Hot

Bad Rap

When you think of holiness, what comes to mind? Thin, hollow-eyed monks with long robes, scraggly beards, and dirty, sandaled feet? Or maybe fasting, rising before dawn to pray, living in rocky deserts, and eating wild locusts? Perhaps your idea is worse than that: Holiness to you equals no jokes, no money, and no sex for your WHOLE LIFE! *Ahhhh!!!*

If this is your sense of holiness, you're not alone. Holiness has gotten a terribly bad rap in today's society. Many non-Christians think of holiness as boring, old-fashioned, and totally undesirable. That's not entirely surprising, since nonbelievers aren't expected to be interested in God's standards of purity.

What may surprise you, however, is how many Christians have the same negative images that nonbelievers do. We think holiness means poverty, bunned hair, and a "holier than thou" attitude.

Let's be honest: None of us wants to marry or date a person who fits that description. You probably wouldn't be thrilled about sharing your life with someone who wears camel skins and takes cold baths.

Fortunately, holiness is not so scary. As believers pursue true holiness (and we'll define it in the next section), they discover that it's the thrilling reality of God living in and through you. Holiness reveals the incredible power of the Holy Spirit in a Christian's life, for only through the work of God can believers attain the unattainable.

Don't make the mistake of believing that holiness is reserved for missionaries, pastors, and pious widows. Holiness is for the day-to-day life of *every* believer, and it should determine the choices Christians make about the people to whom they're drawn.

Uh...Holy?

The simplest definition of *holy* is "sinless." The dictionary further defines it as "spiritually pure" and "dedicated to the service of God." Holiness is the state of being set apart for God and devoted to His purposes. As *holy* synonyms, *Roget's Thesaurus* lists "devout, righteous, godly, moral, just, good, pure, spotless, faultless, upright, virtuous."

But these words, though helpful, cannot encompass the full meaning of holiness. To completely understand the term, we must consider the holiness of God.

God is perfect in holiness. He doesn't merely "live up to the standard." He *is* the standard. Because His very nature is rooted in holiness, He can be no other way. There is no degree of imperfection in Him.

God's holiness is awesome in the truest sense of the word. His righteousness inspires awe because it's so far beyond us. As mortals we can never attain such perfection and purity: God is utterly holy. No wonder the Scriptures call us to praise Him in the beauty and splendor of His holiness (look up 1 Chronicles 16:29 or Psalm 29:2, for example).

In *The Pursuit of God*, A. W. Tozer tells us, "God is holy with an absolute holiness that knows no degrees, and this He cannot impart to His creatures. But there is a relative and contingent holiness...which He has made available to [us] through the blood of the Lamb."[1]

Since God has made holiness available to us, He demands of us a changed life. Holiness cannot remain inactive and dormant. Because holiness is such a significant aspect of His character, God proclaims that it should be a defining trait of His children as well.

Five times—four in the Old Testament and once in the New—God repeats the command "Be holy, because I am holy" (Leviticus 11:44,45; 19:2; 20:7; 1 Peter 1:16). Obviously God considers this an important part of a Christian's life.

Notice that these words from God are an imperative. It's not an option He's merely suggesting—"Be holy if you can" or "Be holy if you feel like it." Holiness is a *must* for all believers all the time.

Secondly, God doesn't say, "Be holy, *as* I am holy." That would be impossible! We can never be as holy as He is. Even the most pure of heart will stumble. We are sinners who live in a fallen world and continue to face temptations, some of which trap us in sin.

The way that Eugene Peterson translates 1 Peter 1:15-16 in *The Message* offers new insight to this command: "As obedient children, let yourselves be pulled into a way of life shaped by God's life, a life energetic and blazing with holiness. God said, 'I am holy; you be holy.'"

It's a simple matter of fact. God is holy; we should be also.

Becoming holy is one of God's ultimate purposes for our lives. "God did not call us to be impure, but to live a holy life" (1 Thessalonians 4:7). He designed us to be holy because we are His, and He is holy. Oswald Chambers emphasizes this truth: "He did not come to save men out of pity; He came to save men because He had created them to be holy."[2]

All for Love

Why does God want us to be holy? We can see the answer in Hebrews 12:14—"Make every effort to live in peace with all men and to be holy; without holiness no one will see the Lord." God created us to be holy because He loves us and wants to live with us eternally, and nothing unholy can remain in His presence. Therefore, all believers who desire to live in and with God must cultivate holiness.

We can be thankful that God took the first step in securing our holiness. He sent His Son to make holiness a possibility for us unholy people. And it's a good thing that He did! Without Jesus, we could never bridge the gap between our sinfulness and God's holiness.

God continues to work holiness in us through the Spirit who dwells in our hearts. This is what Christians call sanctification. It's a process of growth and maturity by which our choices, thoughts, and actions begin to look more and more like God's. He lovingly acts *in* us so that we choose what is holy.

But there's a part *we* must play as well. Jerry Bridges talks about it in his book *The Pursuit of Holiness.* This pursuit, he writes, "is a joint venture between God and the Christian. No one can attain any degree of holiness without God working in his life, but just as surely no one will attain to it without effort on his own part."[3]

Bridges goes on to articulate five essential elements of living out holiness in a practical way: conviction (knowing God's truth), commitment (the willingness to follow those convictions in obedience), discipline (obeying God in our daily choices), dependence (relying on the Spirit rather than our own will power), and desire (longing for God and God alone).

So, to be serious about holiness, a believer needs to know God's love and His Word, to obey His loving commands, to make good choices on a day-to-day basis, to trust in God's power, and to make Him the center of every thought and act.

The more we desire God and love Him, the more we long for holiness in our own lives. In 2 Corinthians 7:1, Paul challenges us with these words: "Let us purify ourselves from everything that contaminates body and spirit, perfecting holiness out of reverence for God." If we revere Him, we will value and pursue holiness.

We've come a long way from the distorted views of holiness that started this chapter. Holiness is by no means boring, but active and alive. Holiness isn't just for some believers, but for all. And holiness doesn't limit us, but instead expands our potential and possibilities. As Tozer says, seeking God (and therefore holiness) "does not narrow one's life, but brings it, rather, to the level of highest possible fulfillment."[4] Holiness is the key to an abundant and full life.

Top of the List

Can you see why holiness is the most fundamental characteristic of a H.O.T. man or woman? When we come face to face with the beauty and splendor of God's holiness, it's hard to want anything less, and in dating and marriage, hard to settle for anything less than a man or woman committed to the pursuit of holiness.

Still not convinced? Then consider the following.

As a Christian, you most likely want to date and eventually marry someone of godly character. That kind of character begins with and centers on holiness. Let me explain.

Imagine for a moment that God had the attributes of love, faithfulness, and grace, but He was *not* holy. In that case, His love wouldn't be "perfectly" unconditional, His faithfulness not "completely" sure, and His grace not "entirely" free. Why? Because

Holiness assures that all He is and does is perfect and just. The attributes of the true and living God are fully complete because of His holiness. Without holiness, His other attributes would be tainted with imperfection. No way would anyone want to serve that kind of God!

Similarly, how could you trust the love and faithfulness of a man or woman without finding in that person the foundation of holiness? Could you believe he or she would live by the standards God has set forth? Could you expect him or her to keep promises? Holiness is the tie that holds other characteristics of godliness together in harmony.

The very origin of the word *holy* shows why it's the most foundational of all character qualities. Coming from the Anglo-Saxon *halig* or *hal*, it literally means "well, whole, healthy." Everything that is holy leads to life, health, and wholeness. All things opposed to holiness lead to death, destruction, and depravity. When faced with a choice between those two options, we'd all certainly prefer relationships that are full of life, health, and wholeness. But we don't always choose those.

In fact, working in youth ministry for several years, we've seen many examples of good and bad relationships. And the relationships in which a Christian settles for someone less than holy are some of the worst.

We watched with grief as a young woman in our youth group dated a guy who wouldn't have known holy from a hole in the ground. Not only had he been arrested on charges of assault, he also pressured Marlene to compromise her standard of sexual purity.

Marlene's parents did their best to intervene and set boundaries, but their daughter ignored the warning signs and continued to sneak around with her boyfriend. Eventually, she stopped coming to church, allowing the destructive relationship to derail her own pursuit of holiness.

Months of fighting with her parents and deceiving them damaged the life, health, and wholeness of Marlene's family. If only she had held out for a relationship with a man devoted to holiness, she wouldn't have hurt her parents and her own relationship with God.

On the other hand, being in a relationship with a holy man or woman will encourage your walk with the Lord. "As iron sharpens iron; so one man sharpens another" (Proverbs 27:17). If you want to sharpen your holy character, spend time with those who are growing in holiness themselves.

Two of our students, Lance and Adrian, had an "iron sharpening iron" type of relationship. They set aside time to study the Word together. They also made it a point to ask how they could pray for each another, and they faithfully took those requests before the Lord. As we watched them grow in personal holiness, we saw how their relationship encouraged their faith.

Seeing God's holiness in another person can refresh a faith that has gone lukewarm. In his book *Knowing God*, J. I. Packer says that knowing Him "is a relationship calculated to thrill a person's heart."⁵ Befriending a holy person can help us see just how thrilling a relationship with God can be.

We recently observed this truth in action during an appreciation service we held for graduating seniors. Nancy, a young woman who had strayed from the Lord, stood to thank two of the seniors for helping to infuse her faith with new passion. She had known them years ago when she had walked with the Lord. When she came back to church, she saw that her childhood friends had stayed strong and committed. Teary-eyed, Nancy recounted how much it meant for her to return and rebuild relationships with those who hadn't walked away. Those friends showed her where she could be and made her desire the kind of holiness that came from being intimate with Jesus.

Finally, joining forces with a person in the pursuit of holiness can allow God's will for His world to be worked out more effectively. Two people genuinely serving the Lord as a team will be able to accomplish more than one person on his own. That's why Ecclesiastes tells us, "Two are better than one, because they have a good return for their work" (4:9). Don't you want to be teamed up with someone who has a burning desire to please God, to do His will, and to see His glory multiplied in all the earth?

So What's Holding Us Back?

If holiness is such an essential quality for Christians to pursue in their own lives and to look for in their companions, why doesn't everyone "just do it"?

For one thing, people cannot attain holiness in three easy steps. Sanctification—growing in holiness—is a process that takes a lifetime; it will never be completed this side of heaven. This fact frustrates our "microwave" society that prefers to solve problems by the time the sixty-second timer goes off.

In *A Long Obedience in the Same Direction,* Eugene Peterson notes how in our world "there is little enthusiasm for the patient acquisition of virtue, little inclination to sign up for a long apprenticeship…called holiness."[6]

People often give up on holiness too quickly. They don't want to wait for improvement. They fear the radical change holiness requires in their lives. Bottom line: They aren't convinced that the end result is worth the effort.

As a young Christian, perhaps just starting out on your journey of faith, you need to believe that holiness is worth the time and energy. You need to trust that your toil and concern will produce a bountiful harvest of spiritual fruit. Moreover, you need to settle for nothing less than a man or woman who shares the same commitment and perseverance.

To have a friend, a companion, and a life partner devoted to holiness will encourage you in the patient acquisition of virtue. He or she can spur you on to love and good deeds, as we're commanded to do for one another in Hebrews 10:24. He or she can help rekindle your desire to grow in grace when coldness and carelessness threaten to extinguish your fire.

You're much more likely to quit if you become involved with

someone who will quickly throw in the towel along the path of holiness. Pursue relationships with Christians who desire to finish strong.

Pick and Choose?

People fail to seek holiness for other reasons as well. Many Christians avoid the pursuit of holiness because they're unwilling to take God as He is and to conform to His standards. They pick and choose which of God's precepts to live by rather than take His whole truth to heart.

Further, many of us prefer to compare ourselves to others and judge our holiness by relative standards. This approach often leads to nothing more than "cultural holiness." People adapt themselves to the standards they see around them—to the behavioral patterns of other Christians or of "good people" who are "more or less" holy.

But this kind of selective holiness misses the boat completely. God has not called us to be like those around us. He hasn't commanded us to be "as good as the next guy." He has charged us to conform to His holy standard, which includes *all* of His precepts and principles. True holiness doesn't pick and choose, or compare itself to anything but the righteousness of God.

Rules or No Rules?

Some believers fail in the pursuit of holiness because they take a formulaic approach to righteousness. They see holiness as a list of

do's and don'ts, and they walk a straight and narrow path of prohi-
bition.

When believers ascribe to this version of holiness, they live like
the Pharisees, who let endless rules and rituals become their gods.
They develop a "holier than thou" attitude that repels not only
other people, but also God Himself. Jesus called the holy-by-
formula Pharisees a "brood of vipers" and "whitewashed tombs"
(Matthew 23:33,27).

Others struggle with holiness because they think living by
grace means taking no personal responsibility for their growth in
righteousness. As we pointed out earlier, however, holiness is a joint
venture with God. He does the lion's share, but we choose to work
with and obey the Holy Spirit who indwells us.

Christians often use the phrase "Let go and let God." This
phrase is meant to encourage a believer to depend on the Lord
alone, but when taken to the extreme it can foster a dangerous attitude. Christians must not believe the lie that any "trying" on their
part contradicts dependence on God. On the contrary, Christians
must live with the attitude "I can do everything through him who
gives me strength" (Philippians 4:13). That means telling yourself,
"I can take responsibility for my thoughts and actions because I
know God works in and with me."

If you're tempted to shirk responsibility in the pursuit of holiness, consider this: "Continue to work out your salvation with
fear and trembling, for it is God who works in you to will and
to act according to his good purpose" (Philippians 2:12-13). This

verse indicates that there are divine and human elements of faith. God acts in believers even to *desire* holiness, and we must "work" *with* God.

Little Sin, Big Sin

Another major barrier to pursuing holiness involves a believer's attitude toward sin. Remember that holiness can be defined as "sinlessness." Consequently, sin destroys holiness. Not just sins like murder and adultery. Any sin, no matter how little, taints holiness.

We get into trouble when we start classifying some sins as worse than others. God makes no distinction between sins. The consequences of some sins are greater than the consequences of others, but compromising on any level means abandoning the pursuit of holiness.

This reality creates stumbling blocks for some believers when it comes to relationships. They see it as a "little" sin to lie to their parents about going on a date before they're allowed. They see it as a "little" sin to go further sexually than they know they should. It's not like I'm going "all the way," they rationalize.

But actually they have gone "all the way." They've gone all the way in trespassing against God's standard of holiness. So often it's "the little foxes that ruin the vineyards" (Song of Songs 2:15). Don't allow the cunning foxes of "little" compromises to spoil your walk with Christ.

Christians cannot categorize sin as "big" or "little" if they're to live holy lives. They must take sin as seriously as the Lord does. He tells us that "the wages of sin is death" (Romans 6:23). He doesn't specify which sin because *all* sin leads to death. We must not compromise with sin.

So proceed with caution! If you begin a relationship with someone who compromises with sin, you will eventually begin to settle for less than God's ultimate standard. If you join forces with a person who sees holiness as a list of do's and don'ts, you risk falling into the trap of legalism. If you build a relationship with someone who compares his or her holiness to others around him, you too will begin to see holiness as merely a relative standard.

As you date, don't settle for anything less than a truly holy individual. You've caught a glimpse of the holiness of God, and you've heard His command to be holy because He is. Now accept His charge to pursue relationships with men and women committed to His standards. Don't be held back by misunderstandings or misperceptions. Press on for holiness—and seek it in others.

Outrageous Is Hot

Uniquely Outrageous

If you haven't picked up on this by now, the *O* in H.O.T. stands for *Outrageous*. But what, you may ask, makes a person outrageous?

Two young women we know exemplify what this word means. Although they are radically different from each other, both are unique, special, and marvelous. Both are outrageous.

Everyone agrees that Megan is one of the brightest lights in her youth group. Her smile is positively contagious, and joy radiates from her. An outstanding athlete, she's strong and tall and energetic. She's always volunteering to serve, whether playing her guitar for worship or heading up the hospitality team. One of the friendliest girls you'll ever meet, Megan is able to put nearly anyone at ease.

Megan may not be what magazines like *Cosmopolitan* would call gorgeous, yet her external and internal beauty combine to make her a truly attractive young woman. In fact, her prom date recently commented that he almost passed out when she walked in the room. What better compliment could a girl get on prom night?

Megan has a vibrant walk with the Lord that flows over into her friendships. Lots of people, guys included, love to be around her. Many quality young men have been drawn to Megan, and part of the reason is that she doesn't realize just how outrageous she is. She's confident without being arrogant, and she's not focused on herself all the time.

Megan would never call herself a H.O.T. woman, but she is!

You may not think this kind of outrageousness is for you. "I'm not outgoing or athletic like that, and I wouldn't really fit with someone who was. Are all H.O.T. individuals just like Megan?" Hardly! Consider Jeni, for example.

Jeni is petite as can be and doesn't usually jump into games like tackle ultimate Frisbee. She's not the athletic type. She sometimes stands to the side, completely absorbed in conversation with someone who's struggling or who just wants to share a laugh. People are drawn to Jeni's sincerity and authenticity. She shows genuine concern and love for others.

She's quieter than many other teenagers and thinks about things on a deeper level than most. Jeni is passionate about reaching out to nonbelievers and those who feel disconnected or rejected. She consistently encourages others to step out of their comfort zones and let God use them to bless those who are hurting.

Jeni's beauty also differs from the fashion magazine models. Yet her eyes sparkle with joy, and her whole face glows when she smiles. She dresses both modestly and attractively and doesn't over-whelm her small and lovely face with too much makeup.

Both girls and guys enjoy spending time with Jeni. She's fun to be with and has friends of all kinds—from crazy, to gothic, to shy as can be. No one feels uncomfortable around her because she is kind and genuinely interested in everyone.

Guys who have been attracted to Jeni are challenged and amazed by her deep devotion to the Lord. She truly walks the walk—and that's very attractive to a young man who desires to pur-sue holiness himself.

Both Jeni and Megan are H.O.T. women who are outrageous in distinct ways. Their examples demonstrate that someone doesn't have to be a certain type to be outrageous.

Can't Forget You

Megan and Jeni help us see what an outrageous person is like, but to pinpoint the true meaning of the word, we need some help.

In our dictionary, the definition of *outrageous* is rather negative. But we want to emphasize the positive connotation this word has assumed in recent years. To most young people, *outrageous* speaks of something shockingly wonderful. So in this book, we're using the word to mean "remarkable, exceptional, extraordinary, special, unique, memorable, wonderful, marvelous, striking, electrifying, and noteworthy." All of God's children are outrageous in their own way because they're unique designs of His creative hand.

Looking back to the examples of Megan and Jeni, you can see why we label them "outrageous." They're remarkable and memorable for their unique and special traits. They're noteworthy for their character and their attractiveness. They're electrifyingly and strikingly fun. All said and done, they're both wonderful and marvelous.

Basically, *outrageous* means "remarkable." Remarkable in some way or another. Remarkable for humor or fun-lovingness. Remarkable for a unique way of dressing or smiling or laughing. Remarkable for unparalleled mercy or kindness. Remarkable for a walk with the Lord that inspires others. There is an infinite number of ways that a person can be remarkable!

And a remarkable person stands out in your memory. In fact, that's exactly what happened to the two of us. Even before we had officially met each other, we each saw something unique and special in the other person. We like thinking back to how we were drawn to each other's outrageous aspects, especially during the early days when both of us were on staff with the First Evangelical Free Church of Fullerton. Join us as we briefly replay a few early memories...

(From Jerusha) There were nearly fifty staff members for our huge Fullerton EV Free youth group, so although Jeramy and I knew of each another, it was awhile before we had any personal interaction.

One summer, Jeramy returned from a two-month mission to

Poland to discover that a chronic sore throat was actually tonsillitis. After his tonsillectomy, when it was time for his Poland team to share their experiences with the rest of the youth group, he was still voiceless. One of my first impressions of Jeramy was watching him in front of the entire youth group that night, unable to utter a single word.

What was so remarkable was the way he could still be so hilarious without a voice. His facial expressions and body language were *so funny.* I laughed with the entire audience at his playful humor and noted in the back of my mind what an outrageous guy he seemed to be.

(From Jeramy) I had actually noticed Jerusha some time before that. In fact, Jerusha first caught my eye two years earlier, on one of the rare occasions when she visited our youth group meeting while home from college.

That night her brother Jonathan and his band Upright were playing for our group, and Jerusha had come to cheer him on. Little did she know that when she walked past her future husband, I turned to ask someone who she was. When she joined the youth group's volunteer staff two years later, I still remembered her. She was unforgettable.

Personality Inside Out

Every one of God's children has the capacity to be outrageous in his or her own way. As unique expressions of God's image, we all have something that makes us outrageously distinct from others. So let's look more closely at some outrageous qualities to help you identify them in others.

Have you ever heard someone say, 'Well, he's not much to look at, but he's got a *great* personality"? Yikes! If you're going to say that about someone, you're better off keeping your mouth shut.

Seriously, though, personality can make or break a person's attractiveness. A great personality attracts, while a bad one repels. If someone is physically striking but totally obnoxious, you can stand that person only for so long. Without an agreeable disposition, a person's good looks will fade fast.

We define *personality* as "the visible aspect of one's character as it impresses others." To understand why personality is so important, let's break that definition down.

For starters, like it or not, character is visible on the outside. If someone is ugly and selfish on the inside, it's eventually going to show on the outside. He may hide it well for a while, but his true colors will come through.

Conversely, if someone is loving and caring, those traits will clearly shine through. People really are made more or less beautiful by their personality. Character is literally visible!

It seems like a no-brainer that people would want to find someone of the opposite sex whose character is attractive, someone whose personality is visibly beautiful. Yet you'd be surprised by how many people think they need to hold out for an outrageous personality only when they want a "serious relationship."

Get real! If someone spends all his or her time vying for the cutest chick or most handsome guy rather than the person with the greatest personality, why would that person's priorities suddenly change when it's time for something more "serious"? What people train themselves to value now *will* stick with them. Don't waste your time with (and definitely don't be) someone who doesn't value a great personality.

The last part of our definition of personality—"as it impresses others"—is also significant. The way we're using *impress* here means more than "to create a favorable image in someone's mind." It means "to affect deeply or strongly, or to establish firmly."

Think for a minute about your own personality. The way your character becomes visible to others will deeply or strongly influence the way they think about you. In anyone's mind, perception is 100 percent reality. It doesn't matter to others if you're different "on the inside." What they see of you determines what they will believe about you. The way you come off will make a lasting impression on a person.

You may be fun loving but use sarcasm to make others laugh. Catch a sensitive person off guard, and you risk giving the impression that you're cruel and unfeeling.

You may be shy and reserved, but if others feel uncomfortable because of your silence, you could be seen as arrogant or self-absorbed.

Character *does* show, and it *does* impact others strongly. But outrageous people focus on keeping their inside attractive rather than on trying to change the way people perceive them. Because their inner quality shines through, their personality makes the right impression the first time.

As a Christian looking for someone to date or eventually marry, don't settle for anything less than someone with a *great* personality. Search for someone who will delight you again and again.

Joy

Something else that always makes a person remarkable or memorable is a genuine, joyful passion for the Lord. What better way to tell if someone is connected with the Savior than by the amount of joy in his or her life?

That assertion may shock you. You may be thinking, "What about looking at how much they read their Bible? Or how much time they devote to prayer or service?"

Many Christians dutifully read the Word and practice disciplines like prayer and service. But how many of them do these things with radiant joy? For those that do, their joy sets them apart.

"So what you're telling me is that being happy all the time is evidence of a dynamic relationship with Jesus?"

No! Happiness and joy are very different things. Happiness may be an expression of joy, but while happiness comes and goes with circumstance, joy remains constant. Joy is the constant delight in our God who is the source of all that is good and praiseworthy and excellent.

Joy comes from the abiding hope that even what is not right

now will eventually be made right in Christ. That's why we're told, "Consider it pure *joy,* my brothers, whenever you face trials of many kinds" (James 1:2). Since joy lasts and enables us to persevere, it's even more remarkable and precious than happiness.

But we Christians sometimes focus so much on the aspects of obedience and righteousness in our walk with Christ that we forget to *delight* in Him. We're like the Israelites of Nehemiah's day, whose despair over their past failures kept them from celebrating what God was doing in their life that very moment. They had become paralyzed and weak in their sorrow. They needed to be renewed by His strength. So Nehemiah stood before the people and proclaimed, "Do not grieve, for the joy of the LORD is your strength" (Nehemiah 8:10).

Eugene Peterson writes that "joy is not a requirement of Christian discipleship, it is a consequence."[1] Even a Christian who sins or faces trials will have joy if he walks with the Lord and trusts in Him. For the believer's strength is not perfection or conviction, but the joy of the Lord.

According to the Westminster Shorter Catechism, our chief purpose in life is to glorify God and enjoy Him forever. If a person enjoys God, he will inevitably find joy in life, because enjoying God means taking joy in the wonderful things that come from Him and through Him.

Joy also improves the lives of those around us. Joy cannot be kept to itself. It must be shared and spread until it consumes gloom and despair. Joy is infectious and wonderfully contagious.

Perhaps this explains why "sense of humor" consistently ranks as one of the top traits people look for in a person of the opposite sex. Godly joy includes the ability to laugh and play and find the humor in life. It's a quality that brings healing to others: "A cheerful heart is good medicine, but a crushed spirit dries up the bones" (Proverbs 17:22). A joyful person is always more fun to be around than a depressed person is.

Think back to the example of both Megan and Jeni. Both of these young women exhibit joy in their own ways. This doesn't mean that they never get sad or face hard things. But the overwhelming pattern of their lives is a display of authentic joy. Strengthened by joy, Megan and Jeni are able to experience life as the delight of God.

In this twisted world, it's easy to focus on the negative, the depressing, and the difficult. Outrageous people, however, know that the joy of the Lord is their strength and, at the same time, strength for others. That knowledge makes them unique and remarkable.

Let's Admit It

When was the last time you heard a pastor say that he married his wife because his heart did backflips when she walked into a room? Or when was the last time you heard a Christian speaker admit that the first thing that drew him to his beloved was her awesome smile and gorgeous blue eyes?

These confessions would be unacceptable in many churches or Christian circles. We expect to hear instead that the pastor married his wife because of her servant leadership or because she knew more Scripture than anyone else he had met. Such reasons seem more noble or more godly. But why is that? Can we truly say that physical appearance doesn't matter to Christians because we're focused only on the heart?

Let's be honest: No way!

Christians *are* attracted by appearance, as well as personality. Believers have eyes too. (*From Jeramy:* Earlier in this chapter, did you catch what I first noticed about Jerusha? It wasn't her amazing devotion to Scripture memory that drew my attention. I *saw* her. Her appearance was uniquely attractive to me. Later I found that her personality accentuated this beauty.)

Christians notice appearances, and it's *not* ungodly! Many biblical characters are noted for their physical attractiveness. Abraham's wife Sarah is called "a very beautiful woman" (Genesis 12:14). When their son Isaac first sees his future wife, Rebekah, she, too, is described as "very beautiful" (24:16). Isaac's son Jacob marries Rachel in part because she is "lovely in form, and beautiful" (29:17). And Jacob's son Joseph is described as "well-built and handsome" (39:6). And that's all in the Bible's first book!

Consider the Song of Solomon (or Song of Songs), which details how two newlyweds are attracted to each other. Hundreds of references are made to the splendor and loveliness of one or the other. The refrain "How beautiful you are, my darling! Oh, how beautiful!" rings throughout the entire text. Clearly these two were not ashamed to be physically attracted to each other!

It's wrong for Christians to assume or pretend that physical attraction isn't important. Physical attraction is part of God's plan to draw husbands and wives to each other. Being physically attracted to someone isn't sinful!

Of course it's possible to go to extremes and focus on physical beauty to the exclusion of other H.O.T. characteristics. Relationships centered on physical attractiveness alone can end quickly because they're based on unbalanced expectations and desires. While there's nothing wrong with being attracted to someone physically, there is something wrong with making that the only or even the biggest requirement for someone of the opposite sex. Physical attraction is only one part of the equation.

Many Christians think of this as an either/or issue—a person is either physically attractive or godly, but not both. In fact, the two of us went through a period of believing that in order to marry a godly mate, we'd have to sacrifice the idea of marrying someone we were physically electrified by.

As if! God showed us how foolish we were to assume that He couldn't combine both outrageous holiness and outrageous attractiveness in a person.

When we held hands for the first time, both of us admitted later that it felt as if a spark shot through our whole body. Reason told us that the air was just dry and static electricity produced the shock. But the next time, same thing! Our electric attraction wasn't a fluke.

God made each of us physically different so we could delight in His infinite creativity and beauty—and so that we could be attracted to one another as individuals. In every person's appearance there is something He created to be praiseworthy and magnetic. It could be the gentle way her hair falls across her face. It could be the unique color or playful dancing of his eyes. It could be a smile that consumes his entire face or the way her grin shyly reveals pure joy. It could be the way her dress complements her skin tone or the way his clothes reflect a fascinating personality.

Every person is God's workmanship, so we can always find something to appreciate in a person's physical appearance. It's not wrong to admit that physical attractiveness is important. But it needs to be kept in balance with the other aspects of a H.O.T. person.

Discovering the Outrageous

A few things to wrap up before we move on to the last H.O.T. characteristic...

First, holiness and outrageousness go hand in hand. A righteous person can be just as passionate and fun as anyone. Holy doesn't mean boring, and outrageous doesn't mean wild. The two are complementary in the Christian who loves and knows the Lord.

Second, don't feel bad for wanting someone with outrageous qualities. Though some Christians may downplay or ignore the significance of fun or physical attraction in a relationship, these traits can be vitally important. The key is to keep your desire for them in balance with your desire for other qualities.

Finally, this special note: Sometimes it takes time and effort to develop your outrageous qualities. Keep that in mind if you ever feel you aren't remarkable in any way.

You may already have an idea of what some of your outrageous traits are. If so, work on them to make them the best they can be. You may skateboard or dance extraordinarily well. Develop that skill and see if you don't find someone who appreciates your unique talent.

You may be a good listener or be able to make others laugh. Reveal those qualities to others in a genuine way. Let them see the real you. You may know how to dress well or how to do your hair in just the perfect way. Even recognizing the simplest of things can make you feel more outrageous. When you develop and appreciate the outrageous qualities in yourself, you'll eventually catch the eyes of others.

Sometimes you may need someone else to help you realize your outrageous qualities. If you don't have a clue about what makes you remarkable, ask others you trust to help you figure it out. Have them help you accentuate the best and most unique things about you. Not only will this show you how special and remarkable you are, but it will allow others to see this as well.

Some people have an easier time expressing their outrageous qualities than others do. But all Christians should find—and be— outrageously H.O.T. individuals!

4

Trustworthy Is Hot

Sudden Shock

Imagine meeting the man or woman of your dreams—someone gorgeous, easy to talk to, sensitive, and fun. You date, and eventually that moment comes when the question is popped and the wedding bells begin to chime. You can't believe it's really happening, and you're dazed with fairy-tale happiness.

Now imagine "waking up" sometime later to find that Mr. or Mrs. Right is not so right after all. Your spouse begins to lie to you, and when you confront him or her about it, more deceit follows. It gets so bad that ultimately the relationship falls apart, and separation appears to be the only option.

Suddenly you're alone again, not fully understanding what happened. Slowly you try to piece together what's left of your life, but your shattered heart aches with the realization that you relied on someone unworthy of your trust.

You may think this is an extreme example, but sadly, it's very close to the story of a couple we knew. We didn't suspect a thing until Garret and Becky's marriage was already in shambles. We thought we had no reason to worry about those two.

Garret and Becky seemed as perfect a couple as you could find. Both were tremendously attractive people, and they just seemed to belong together, like Ken and Barbie.

They enjoyed outdoor activities and drove a Chevy Blazer long before SUVs populated the entire planet. They had no children, but those of us on the outside thought it could only be a matter of time before their beautiful babies would start to arrive.

What made Garret and Becky even more "perfect" was their devotion to working with young people. They loved serving in their church and spent countless hours organizing spectacular youth events. Their magnetic personalities and fun-loving spirits drew all kinds of kids who wouldn't normally darken the door of a church.

Parents counted themselves lucky to be able to send their children into Garret and Becky's program, and kids looked forward to when they would *finally* be allowed to join the beach volleyball games and pizza parties.

A couple of years into Garret and Becky's marriage, difficult issues started to surface. At first there were just rumors of indiscretion. Those of us who loved the couple vehemently defended our beloved friends against what we thought was slanderous gossip.

Then Garret disappeared. We learned that he and Becky had chosen to separate and that divorce was hovering in the all-too-near future. Their entire church was devastated. Young people were disillusioned, and parents were outraged. Many questioned how they could stay in a church that had trusted "such people" with their children.

Church members quickly found out why Garret left. Not only had he been unfaithful to his wife multiple times, but he had also taken advantage of several of the students under his care. Ultimately we discovered that Garret had become addicted to pornography and had refused Becky's many attempts to seek counseling.

Garret broke trust on many levels. First and foremost, he betrayed his Lord. He destroyed the trust that his friends and his church had placed in him. He also painfully and horribly ravaged his wife's trust. Garret broke faith with the woman whom he had vowed to love, protect, and cherish. Alone and afraid, Becky had to consider how she could have believed in such a fake, such a liar.

He had pretended to love Jesus. He had feigned loving Becky. His deceptions were so deep that he denied his problems while running time and again to pornography, the idol that he'd chosen as his lover.

All of us who knew Garret and Becky felt betrayed by him in many ways, but our deepest grief couldn't compare to Becky's. She had given Garret her whole heart, only to have it crushed by his infidelity and deceit.

Honest to God

Years later, Becky admitted that even before she married Garret she saw signs that he wasn't completely trustworthy. Sometimes his stories just didn't add up. He wouldn't follow through on commitments, and often he showed more interest in his own desires than in hers.

Young and in love, Becky believed these weaknesses could be overlooked. Naively she assumed that by living with and loving him she could eventually change some of these things in Garret. But the truth was that she could never make Garret trustworthy.

Can you imagine how much Becky, looking back, wishes that she had broken off their relationship before they were married? And how much she wishes she had waited for someone trustworthy?

How about you? Do you even know how to recognize what makes a person worthy of trust? To avoid the kind of suffering Becky endured, you need to learn how to identify a trustworthy person.

God is the ultimate standard of trustworthiness; He never falters and never changes. The prayer in Psalm 9:10 reveals this with brilliant clarity: "Those who know your name will trust in you, for you, LORD, have never forsaken those who seek you." *Never* forsaken! We can have complete confidence in the Lord because He has proven Himself to be utterly dependable and trustworthy.

The world tells you to trust no one but yourself, since the

human race is unreliable, unpredictable, and prone to deceit. Even in Shakespeare's time this advice was given: "Trust none; for oaths are straws, men's faiths are wafer-cakes."[1]

Yet any lasting relationship, especially marriage, demands a high level of trust. Being married to someone you couldn't trust would be frightening. You would always wonder if your spouse was telling you the truth and if he or she was being faithful to you alone. You'd never know if your heart was safe.

Sadly, too many married people live in such fear. Sometimes the partners try to protect themselves from heartbreak by staying emotionally distant from each other; sometimes they just keep getting their heart broken, always taking the risk to trust again with no guarantees that this time will be different.

Christians shouldn't live with such fear. Trusting our hearts to God, and pursuing relationships with others who trust Him, should give us a level of confidence in relationships. Even if our heart gets broken, there's Someone who will always be worthy of our trust. God, the Lover of our souls, *can* be trusted. And a person devoted to Christ can say, "My flesh and my heart may fail, but God is the strength of my heart and my portion forever" (Psalm 73:26).

Trusting someone who is trusting God is safer and easier than trusting someone who is not. People who have surrendered to Christ aren't perfect, but they show themselves worthy of trust by their authentic, honest, and reliable lifestyle.

You're Not Fooling Anyone...

Authentic, honest, reliable. These are the three defining characteristics of a trustworthy person. What do they mean?

Authenticity speaks of a genuine disposition as well as a life that shows consistency.

An old saying goes something like "Judge a man by the rule of his life, not by the exception." All humans will sin and act inconsistently with their beliefs at one time or another. But the pattern of a person's life helps you determine whether he or she is genuinely worthy of your trust.

A few months ago, a young man began coming to our youth group. He said that God had rescued him from the party scene and completely turned his life around. Naturally, we were thrilled and thankful to the Lord.

Austin went on some youth events and even asked if he could get involved in the high-school leadership. But entrusting him with that responsibility just didn't seem wise at the time; Austin hadn't yet shown enough of a pattern of authentic and consistent discipleship to put him in front of the group as a leader.

Later we were glad we had made that decision. We discovered that, within a week, Austin had asked out three different girls in the youth group and made some of them uncomfortable with his aggressive manner. We wondered if his words about a "changed life" were meant more to snag girls than to honor the Lord. Thankfully, those young women had enough discernment to turn him down, having sensed that his life didn't match his words.

A big part of authenticity is simply being the person you claim to be. Austin claimed to be changed, but his actions showed otherwise. His life proved inconsistent, which made it impossible for him to be genuine and real.

In *The Calvary Road,* Roy Hession says, "The first effect of sin in us is always to make us hide; with the result that we're pretending, we're wearing a mask, we aren't real with either God or man. And, of course, neither God nor man can fellowship with an unreal person."[2]

Those young women couldn't have had true fellowship with Austin because he hadn't proven authentic or real. He hid sin behind a mask. Had Austin been more real about who he was and where he was with God, over time he might have truly changed and rightfully earned people's trust.

Finding a trustworthy person means finding someone whose actions match his words. It means waiting for someone who proves real and consistent with the Lord and with you.

Liar, Liar

On his first day on the job after passing the bar exam, a young attorney began setting up his new office, arranging everything from his nameplate on the door to the frame around his law degree. When all was neatly in place, he sat down behind his empty desk, worrying about how he'd acquire his first client.

It wasn't long before footsteps echoed on the hall floor, and his excitement rose.

Suddenly he realized the peril of having this potential client think that he was a rookie. He grabbed for the phone and began dramatically talking to the dead line: "Why of course! I *am* an experienced litigator. In fact, I've tried several similar cases."

The footsteps came closer.

"I specialize in a variety of legal affairs," the new lawyer continued, "and I happen to know my prices are competitive with every major firm in town. After all, one can never do too much for his client." He laughed a hard, coarse laugh, the kind he thought lawyers were supposed to have.

Finally, the footsteps halted at his door, and a slight rap on the wooden frame sent his pulse racing. His first customer!

Placing his hand over the phone, he politely called, "Come in."

The door opened. A somewhat dingily dressed man in blue coveralls and a baseball cap stood there. *Well,* the young lawyer thought, *not necessarily a dream client, but everyone's got to start somewhere.*

"Can I help you?" he said in a practiced legal tone.

"Sure can," the man smiled knowingly. "I'm from the telephone company, and I'm here to hook up your phone."

Bummer!

But think of this: Suppose the footsteps *had* been those of a potential client. Maybe she would have been impressed by the show and decided to hire the lawyer. Then consider her anger and disillusionment upon finding out later, as she no doubt would, that he had deceived her. Do you think she would be angry enough to demand her money back before storming out on him? Sure she would. How could she ever trust someone like that?

Now suppose the lawyer had been committed to honesty. The telephone guy who entered the empty office and met the eager young attorney might have known of someone who needed legal counsel, or perhaps he needed some legal work himself. Unfortunately the humiliated attorney never found out what honesty could have led to.

Honesty is often a lot harder than deceit. But for Christians, there's never an excuse for dishonesty.

As David reminds us in Psalm 51:6, God desires truth in our inner beings. Proverbs 12:22 is even more direct: "The LORD detests lying lips, but he delights in men who are truthful." That word *detests* is pretty strong. The Lord despises dishonesty; He is repulsed by it.

In accordance with God's values, Christians should not maintain relationships with people who repeatedly lie and deceive. Instead, make connections with H.O.T. people who are trustworthy because they're authentic and honest. Don't get involved with someone who *habitually* falsifies the truth. Honest people show a greater pattern of truthfulness that eclipses any mistakes they may make.

(*From Jeramy:* When we were dating, Jerusha once came to me and admitted that she'd told me a lie. [We tried and tried to remember what it was as we outlined this chapter, but to no avail!] She felt terrible, and it showed in her face. I was overwhelmed that our relationship was so important to her that she was willing to confess her sin and face the consequences. I knew that the pattern of Jerusha's life was one of honesty, so I didn't hesitate to forgive her and to keep moving forward in our relationship. In fact, her confession strengthened my trust in her. I knew that if we could be honest with each other, even about our mistakes, the trustworthiness of our relationship was secure.)

But You Said You Would!

There's nothing worse than flaky people, especially when you've counted on them to hold up their end of a project, task, or bargain. When they let you down, you feel misled, deluded, and maybe more than a little angry. How could they not follow through?

The third fundamental characteristic of trustworthy people is that they're reliable. They don't flake. They do what they say they'll do. You can count on reliable people; you don't have to wonder if they'll come through. They call when they say they'll call. They're there when they promise to be. They do what they've vowed to do.

Imagine how you'd feel in this situation: Judy had dated a few times during high school, but had never been in what she'd call a "real relationship." It's not that she didn't want one; she would have given her right arm to know the romance of holding hands in the school hallways or slow dancing at homecoming. It just never seemed to happen for Judy.

In her last year of high school, she dreaded the senior prom. At her school, anybody who was anybody went to prom. The girls spent hours selecting expensive dresses and perfectly coiffuring their hair. The guys rented the latest Michael Jordan tuxes, and some even sprung for limos to transport their dates to the dance in style.

Judy didn't expect anyone to ask her. She had a few good guy friends, but they all had dates with someone else a month before the dance. She was resigned to spending another Saturday night watching *Sleepless in Seattle* with her cat. She tried to ignore the chatter of her friends about who was wearing what and where everyone planned to go for dinner.

When the big dance was only two days away, Tyler sat down next to Judy at lunchtime in the cafeteria. She and Ty had been buds since before she could remember, and they talked about everything. Judy had deep affection for her friend, but she kept her feelings hidden so no one suspected anything more than a friendship.

Ty wasn't himself that day. His eyes seemed dull, and his strong shoulders were slumped. Judy soon found out why. His girlfriend had broken up with him the night before and told him she wouldn't go to the prom with him. It was too late for Ty to get a refund for the tickets he'd bought or to cancel the limo he'd rented. On top of the pain of a broken relationship, he faced losing a hundred and fifty bucks on a non-prom.

Judy listened quietly and squeezed Ty's hand. Finally she said, "She's crazy to break it off with you. Being your prom date would have been such an honor."

Ty looked at her for a second without saying anything, but Judy could tell he was thinking. Suddenly, as if a light had gone on in his head, he blurted out, "Well, why can't you be my date? I've already got everything set. What do you think?"

"Seriously?"

"Completely," he answered. "Judy, would you please go to prom with me?"

Stunned, but happier than she had been in a long time, Judy couldn't answer him. She just sat there in silence. Finally Ty caught her attention with a "Well?" kind of gaze.

"Yeah," she declared. "I will."

For Judy, the next two days were a frenzy of shopping and preparations and pinching herself to see if she was dreaming. By Saturday morning, a gorgeous gown was hanging in her closet, and in her heart there was a confidence that this really wasn't a dream— just a dream-come-true.

Around 11 A.M., just as she was about to leave for appointments to have her hair and nails done, the phone rang. Her little brother yelled up the stairs in a mocking tone, "Judy, it's a BOY."

I hope Ty didn't hear that, she thought.

She picked up the receiver to hear Ty's familiar voice: "Hey, what's up?"

"Not much," she replied reservedly, suppressing the flutter she felt inside just hearing his voice.

"Uh, Judy," he began, "I have something to ask you." He sounded nervous, maybe even upset. "Well, uh—Lori called me last night, and we decided to get back together. And, well, I was sorta wondering if you'd mind if I took her to the prom like I'd planned to."

Judy felt her face burning and a sob welling up inside her. *How could he do this?*

Somehow words came out of her mouth. "No…I don't mind. I guess that's cool." Quickly, she followed up with, "Well, I better go. I have to take care of some things. I hope you guys have a really good time."

"I'm so glad you understand," she heard him say. "I knew I could count on you. See ya Monday, okay?"

When the line went dead, Judy let herself break down. She cried for hours. Her mom tried to console her by taking her out that night for her favorite Mexican dinner, but when they entered the restaurant and saw some high-school couples there, she asked if they could just go home.

Understandably, Judy had a hard time trusting guys for the next few years. She didn't think she could rely on anyone. If such a close friend would actually do this to her, why wouldn't all guys? She just didn't believe anyone would follow through.

Judy eventually met and married a godly and trustworthy man. But first he had to show her again and again that he was reliable and could be trusted. It took a long time for her broken trust to heal.

Finding someone you can count on, someone you can trust to follow through, is absolutely essential in developing a healthy relationship. To avoid a painful situation like Judy's, develop relationships with people who keep their word and fulfill their promises.

Fragile—Handle with Care

But how do you know if someone is trustworthy enough to be careful with your heart, the most precious "wellspring of life"? (Proverbs 4:23). Can someone be authentic and honest and reliable—and yet still break your heart?

Most of the time, no. But there are some people who exhibit strong personal integrity—an apparent commitment to morality and truth—and yet have little concern for the hearts of others. So how can you determine if a person is trustworthy enough when it comes to your heart?

To tell whether a person is worthy of your heart's trust, observe him or her in a variety of circumstances. You may have seen someone extraordinarily reliable in a crisis, but to give that person your heart, you need to see that he or she is consistently faithful in day-to-day things as well.

Oswald Chambers expresses it this way: "The test of a man's...character is not what he does in the exceptional moments of life, but what he does in the ordinary times, when there is nothing tremendous or exciting [going] on."[3] To be faithful with something as valuable as your heart, a person must show faithfulness with smaller things. As Jesus said, "Whoever can be trusted with very little can also be trusted with much, and whoever is dishonest with very little will also be dishonest with much" (Luke 16:10).

Examine people in the ordinary situations of life to determine if they're faithful with the "very little." If they aren't, don't assume that they'll be faithful with your heart.

Another way to tell if someone would be trustworthy with your heart is to look at that person's relationship with the Lord. Is he or she sensitive to how sin grieves God's heart? Is that person in tune with God's commands and desires and plans?

Look also at his or her relationships with other people, especially family members. Does this person treat family members' hearts with love and concern? If not, chances are he or she will eventually treat you with the same disregard.

Finally, look for consistency in how this person treats you. If there are moments of controlling or selfish behavior, chances are things won't improve much the deeper your relationship goes.

Also take notice of how much concern this person shows for the things that matter to you. Do you see a willingness to learn about your interests? (*From Jeramy:* This may sound silly to you, but one of the ways Jerusha knew I was interested in the things she liked was that I watched Laker basketball games with her. I started to know the team and cheer along with her. That simple thing built a bond between us because I demonstrated that what mattered to her mattered to me.)

People who are trustworthy with your heart will protect

you, shielding you from pain whenever possible. They will respect your emotional and physical comfort level and not push you beyond that. In a dating relationship, they will also help you guard your heart to protect you from excessive pain if you should break up.

Finally, people who will be trustworthy with your heart should have personal integrity as well. Their life will show the traits of authenticity, honesty, and reliability. You can trust these kinds of people in all situations because they have shown themselves to be deserving of your confidence.

If You Happen to Choose Poorly...

What are the consequences of relying on someone unworthy of your trust? They can range from relatively minor to positively agonizing.

You may be like Lloyd Dobler, hero of the classic eighties' film *Say Anything*. He falls in love with Diane Court, a "valedictorian trapped in the body of a game show hostess." Later she breaks off their relationship, leaving him with a parting gift. In shock he tells a friend, "I gave her my heart and she gave me a pen." Kinda funny, kinda sad.

Or you may be like Mandy, a girl in our youth group who recently lamented that the guy she had been seeing for some time was now ignoring her completely. She tried to joke with us: "Yeah, I love crying myself to sleep every night." But the pain in her voice was too real to be funny.

Or you may be like the two of us—each of whom suffered from an untrustworthy relationship during high school. In both cases, the person we were dating was not being honest with us. We know personally how that kind of broken trust brings hurt and confusion, tearing you apart.

If you end up marrying someone unworthy of your trust, you're likely to face the ultimate consequences of separation and divorce. The deep wounds heal only slowly and painfully.

It's just not worth it to get involved with someone who doesn't show himself or herself to be authentic, honest, reliable, and trustworthy with your heart. For your own sake, settle for nothing less than a person who puts the *trustworthy* in H.O.T.

The End of the Matter

Even the best of humans, however, will never be perfectly trustworthy. No one except God Himself is perfectly worthy of your trust. There's no shadow of turning with Him, and you can rely on Him for all things in all situations.

And we can be thankful that because God has chosen to live in and through us, we *can* trust believers who follow His example. It's a lot safer and easier to trust someone who is trusting Christ than to trust someone who isn't. Those who truly rely on the Lord will be growing in each of these areas of trustworthiness, and their lives will demonstrate that they are people you can date and eventually marry, confident that they are trustworthy.

He's H.O.T.

From Jeramy

The World's Hottest Men

Recently, while waiting for another program to start, Jerusha and I caught the last five minutes of a television newsmagazine called *Extra*.

The program's final story that night was about the Latino singer Ricky Martin. But the story didn't focus on either his popular music or his many awards and accomplishments. No, this "news" was much hotter—*Extra* had caught Ricky Martin with his shirt off (gasp!) while he was vacationing in Hawaii. No kidding! They built an entire story on that fact, throwing in terribly witty comments like "he showed he's sure in shape" plus images of some native girls cooing and fawning from the shore.

We watched for a moment before both of us burst out laughing. The whole thing seemed so bizarre. Though Martin enjoys teenage heartthrob status, it seemed so ridiculous for a TV program to make such a big deal about him taking off his shirt. Give us a break.

The American media have helped create a national obsession for "hot" men. Each year, *People* magazine announces their choice for "Sexiest Man Alive" in what proves to be one of their top-selling issues. Photos of toned and chiseled men are also featured in their "Fifty Most Beautiful People" issue, along with inane captions that tell us, "He finds the most romantic time of day is sunset" or "He likes to drive up the California coast in his Ferrari." Sometimes there's mention of the charity work or political interests of these "sexiest" or "most beautiful" men, but most of what we're told about them has to do with their physical traits or material possessions. That's what makes these guys hot.

Hollywood turns up the heat even more, giving male hunks plenty of opportunities to show off not only their strength and their toys, but also their courage, ingenuity, and humor. Perhaps Hollywood's all-time classic hot man is James Bond, a character who's been brought to life by four different actors since the first 007 flicks made him an international symbol of sexual prowess and glamour. He remains as popular as ever, his legend still packing eager women into movie houses. The cool quickness, the accent, the tuxedos, the charm—Bond seems to have it all.

And yet the guy's a jerk. He hops from bed to bed, never committing to any one woman. He treats people around him with disdain and condescension. "I'm always right" is his attitude. On top of all that, he's completely chauvinistic. How politically incorrect can one man get?

So why is Bond accepted and even loved by the public? Because his physical attractiveness and allure have been idealized. Men want to be like him; women just want him.

But for those who don't like Bond, the world offers other radically different versions of the hot man. During the nineties, for example, young people began to idolize the stars of grunge bands—guys who were poorly dressed, shaggily groomed, yet enigmatic and intriguing, so into the limelight and onto the magazine covers they went. It was a whole new standard for what's hot: raging tempers, drug addictions, and crimes against the "establishment."

One of the grunge movement's founding fathers was Kurt Cobain. When he shot himself, millions grieved his death. Sympathy T-shirts worn by loving fans made Cobain out to be a hero. His name, his life, and ultimately his death became hotter than hot.

For a moment, imagine that you didn't know the Lord and that guys like James Bond or Kurt Cobain were your only examples of hot masculinity. These were the men you were taught to esteem and revere by the society that idolized them. And if you're a guy, you'd probably try to be a lot like one of them.

As a result, you would likely end up with a promiscuous and shallow life, having no idea how to treat a woman and no clue how to stand for anything of significance. You might wind up obsessed with your own hotness and unable to see beyond yourself to the needs of others.

If that's the likely outcome of following the world's definition of *hot*, do you really want anything to do with it? If not, then where can you turn for a more discerning and balanced view of what's hot? In our experience, the best place is the Word of God. If you want examples of courageous men, the Bible's got them. If you want to see men who love deeply and love well, the biblical stories provide those heroes too. If you want to know about hot men who lead, inspire, and set themselves apart, the Bible highlights many role models.

So let's look at the best in manly characteristics as the Lord defines them. Though the traits we outline in this chapter don't exhaust the biblical ideal of manhood, we're confident they form a good basis for determining which men are really H.O.T.

Setting the Bar High

By now you know that the *H* in H.O.T. is for *Holiness*. Though holiness applies to both men and women, there are some distinct ways that God allows and commands men to live according to His standards for holy living. And those standards are rooted in God's plan for creation.

Long before sin polluted the world, God's plan was for two separate and equal sexes to mirror His image in particular ways. The Lord designed men and women to perform unique tasks and play certain roles within the church and family. Because of their individual makeups, men and women have the opportunity to serve in diverse ways.

One of the ways that men emulate God is through leadership. God designed men to head the church and the family, to lead others by first serving them. If this idea is new to you, check out chapter 13 in our book *I Gave Dating a Chance* where we give an overview of the biblical concept of masculinity. (For more information on what it means to be a godly man, look at such fine books as Stu Weber's *Tender Warrior* or Elisabeth Elliot's *The Mark of a Man*. Both set forth the concepts of biblical manhood with excellent scriptural support.)

The truly H.O.T. man knows and understands his unique and God-given role, and his holiness clearly and distinctly reflects the heart of God. First of all, the holy man upholds righteousness. He stands for what is true and right, even if doing so causes him pain. He doesn't back down or surrender, even though he may stand alone. A holy man is completely devoted to his biblical convictions and acts accordingly.

In Ezekiel 22:30, God speaks of a time when He was looking for such a man among His people, the Israelites: "I looked for a man among them who would build up the wall and stand before me in the gap on behalf of the land so I would not have to destroy it, but I found none." Today God still searches for men who will stand "in the gap"—those who stand up self-sacrificially for integrity, righteousness, and holiness. If you're a man, could God look at you now and find you standing for righteousness at school, at work, and at home? Do you uphold that which is true and defend that which is right? Would God identify you as a man willing to "stand in the gap"?

There are few things women admire more in a man than true courage, the kind of courage that willingly stands up for what's true. Perhaps this appeal exists because God intended men to model bravery and valor. (And since He wants men to stand for righteousness, perhaps that's why He created women with the desire to see them do so.)

The Lord longs to find men who will rise up to defend holiness. He wants men who will uphold righteousness by standing in the gaps. May He never again be disappointed when He searches for such men.

The world needs men who will not lose their individuality to please the crowd, who will make no compromise with unrighteousness, and who aren't embarrassed to speak the truth even when it's unpopular. The world needs men who can say no and mean it, even if the rest of the world screams yes. The world doesn't need more glamorous, bare-chested stars. It needs men of personal and public holiness who will stand for what's right.

To stand for truth, a holy man must first know the truth. He needs to be so immersed in the Word of God that when falsity rears its head, he can defend what he knows is right and genuine.

Paul's words to Timothy are a stirring challenge for every Christian man: "Do your best to present yourself to God as one approved, a workman who does not need to be ashamed and who correctly handles the word of truth" (2 Timothy 2:15). Only a man who accurately handles the word of truth can effectively defend it. If you boldly stand for what you believe, yet those beliefs aren't grounded in the ultimate truth of Scripture, you're standing on shifting sand. Truth, rock-solid truth, comes only from the Word of God, and the holy man appreciates and absorbs that truth. When the time then comes to defend and uphold righteousness, he can show himself approved and capable.

Another fundamental trait of a man committed to holiness is that he applies God's Word to himself before he preaches it to others. He lets the Lord's truth change him before he tries to inspire others to change. Living what he's learned and what he wants to teach protects him from the charge of inauthenticity. Nothing gives leaders a worse reputation than hypocrisy.

Ezra, the Old Testament prophet, exemplified this trait of holiness. Ezra knew the Law and lived by it. Because of his devotion, God called and enabled him to lead the Israelites back to their beloved homeland after being held captive in Babylon. More importantly, the Lord allowed Ezra to lead a spiritual revival, which brought God's children back to the heart of worship. "The gracious hand of his God was on him," we read in Ezra's story, and we quickly see why: "For Ezra had devoted himself to the study and observance of the Law of the LORD, and to teaching its decrees and laws in Israel" (Ezra 7:9-10).

This man of God had his priorities in order. Ezra faced the

monumental task of supervising Jerusalem's reconstruction and the even greater challenge of rekindling the dying spiritual fire of an entire nation. Ezra had been called to lead the children of God in holy truth. To accomplish this, he knew he had to rely on God's Word and God's strength working through him. He couldn't lead without first allowing God to teach him, mold him, and penetrate his life with the truth he was to teach.

Ezra allowed God to refine him first, that he might be a man above reproach. His leadership inspired confidence because the Israelites saw God's heart reflected in Ezra's holiness. His authentic devotion inspired others.

A man cannot be entrusted with the leadership of others until he first applies God's Word to his own life. God wants genuine leaders, not hypocrites who tell everyone else to do what they're not doing. An authentic leader is a H.O.T. man who can lead and inspire confidence by his example. Men and women alike admire and are drawn to such leaders whose daily life matches their proclamation of truth.

Ezra's example also shows us that a holy man is one who leads others in knowing and understanding the person of God. Another Old Testament example of this is the story of Judah's King Josiah.

Josiah became king during a dark period in his nation's history. The Book of the Law had been lost and forgotten. It was discovered by workmen who were repairing the temple in Jerusalem, and the unearthed scrolls were brought to the king and read aloud to him. As he listened to God's words, the king tore his robes and wept over the condition of his country. Appalled by his own sinfulness and the sinfulness of his people, Josiah demonstrated true leadership by responding immediately. We read in 2 Kings 23 how he gathered all the people at the temple and read to them himself from God's Word: "The king stood by the pillar and renewed the covenant in the presence of the LORD—to follow the LORD and keep his commands, regulations and decrees with all his heart and all his soul, thus confirming the words of the covenant written in this book. Then all the people pledged themselves to the covenant" (verse 3).

A true leader won't remain satisfied with simply knowing the truth or even grieving over the consequences of sin. A genuine leader will be motivated to change, and will inspire others to alter their lives as well. Because Josiah chose to make a public stand and gathered the entire nation to witness his promise, he inspired the people to recommit their lives as well.

Isn't it amazing that "*all* the people" followed Josiah's leadership and pledged themselves to the covenant? The example of one man standing for righteousness and applying God's truth to his own life spurred an entire nation to repentance and renewed holiness. Wouldn't you like to follow such an example?

That opportunity is indeed yours. You can be like Ezra and like Josiah. Your commitment to holiness can encourage others to pursue a life that reflects God's standards.

The Outrageous Man

What is it that truly sets a man apart from all the millions of guys on the planet? What makes him remarkable, unique, extraordinary?

Here's a hint: It's not ultimately his Porsche or his hot body. Cars eventually wear out and rust. And even hot bods will wrinkle, sag, and lose their youthful vitality.

But the traits that truly distinguish a man and make him outrageous last forever. These characteristics set him apart for eternity, not just the moment.

Kindness is one of those traits. Because many people don't associate men with kindness, those who display it distinguish themselves as unique and remarkable. Kindness, in both word and deed, truly sets a man apart.

One way that outrageous men show kindness is through common courtesies, such as opening doors for ladies or allowing them to go first in line. Many men do these things at the beginning of a relationship, but then let them slide later as they get comfortable. A truly kind man, however, will keep demonstrating his respect for women.

Allow me to offer another example. My wife hates to clean bathrooms. Though she does it (and does it well, I might add), it isn't a task she looks forward to. One way I show her kindness is to surprise her by cleaning the bathrooms. Trust me, her grateful reaction is worth the effort!

Another way a man can show kindness is by complimenting a woman on her accomplishments or appearance. Even better is to encourage a woman with regard to her character or personality. Expressing words of affirmation sets men apart.

Men often think kind and complimentary thoughts, but don't verbalize them. Few men know how to give a real compliment, yet women crave the encouragement of their male friends and companions. A kind man knows that his words can encourage and uplift others.

And kindness differs from flattery. A flatterer compliments in order to get something from a woman. A man of kindness, on the other hand, expresses genuine appreciation for a woman with words that are true and from the heart.

Men of kindness also show sensitivity to a woman's emotions, even when they don't understand them. I remember when I first discovered my wife was terrified of murder movies. We had gone with some friends to see a terror flick at the dollar theater, and she spent the entire two hours either buried in my sleeve or watching through her hands.

I thought it kind of silly until later that night. After sleeping peacefully for several hours, I awoke to my frightened wife begging me to pray with her. She had been up all night, struggling with the images she had seen on screen. Part of me wanted to say, "You've got to be kidding." As a man, my logical, it's-not-real-so-don't-worry-about-it mentality threatened to take over and "solve" her problem. But at that moment, all my wife wanted and needed was a little kindness—a hug and a prayer and my support. My being sensitive to her emotions made her feel safe and loved.

Such forms of kindness don't come easily for some men. It may seem like a hassle to open her door every time, especially when it's raining or cold. Expressing compliments may sometimes make you feel uncomfortable or silly. Just sensitively "being there" for her may seem impractical. But learning the art of kindness truly sets a man apart as outrageous.

Another identifying trait of an outrageous man is unselfishness, something that is rarely modeled for men in movies, television, or music. Instead, men are urged to look out for numero uno—which is easy for us to do, since selfishness resonates with everything in our flesh.

A truly outrageous man, however, puts the needs and wants of others above his own desires. In *They Call Me Coach,* legendary UCLA basketball coach John Wooden defines a gentleman as "one who considers the rights of others before his own feelings and the feelings of others before his own rights." In short, a gentleman acts and loves unselfishly.

The ultimate example of unselfishness is none other than Christ Jesus Himself, who "did not come to be served, but to serve, and to give his life as a ransom for many" (Matthew 20:28). The King of heaven came down and served. He unselfishly placed us above Himself and loved us without thought for His own well-being. He loved us so much that He gave up His life for us.

Jesus both commands and enables men to follow His example and unselfishly lay down their rights and feelings for others. Doing so sets men apart and makes them different from the "me-deep" world.

Still another countercultural trait of an outrageous man is humility. Once again, Jesus is the ultimate example. God tells us, "Your attitude should be the same as that of Christ Jesus: Who, being in very nature God, did not consider equality with God something to be grasped, but made himself nothing.... He humbled himself and became obedient to death—even death on a cross!" (Philippians 2:5-8).

That's a long way from the prevalent stereotype of the proud and arrogant male. Men struggle with self-absorption. But Jesus calls us to be different, distinct. He calls us to humility, to the losing of our "self."

In fact, true love demands such an attitude of humility. As Mike Mason relates in *The Mystery of Marriage,* "Love, building up and celebrating life, specializes in the destruction of something far more powerful and unyielding than life itself, and that is the human ego." Our egos can be stubborn and unrelenting. We desperately cling to whatever we think we can control. Yet if we're to be men who love and are loved, we must be willing to lay down our life in humility.

You may fear the consequences of this kind of humility. But consider this: In return, you receive not only respect and acceptance, but also the awe and adoration of the woman who loves you back. We always find our truest fulfillment when we're busy losing ourselves in others. That's why Jesus tells us, "Whoever finds his life will lose it, and whoever loses his life for my sake will find it" (Matthew 10:39).

Humility makes a man noteworthy and remarkable. It is also indicative of wisdom, for in true humility we recognize that we don't know it all, can't fix it all, and can never keep it all together. Humility realizes our need for others, and this authenticity attracts others.

Does all this sound like a tall order? Remember that Jesus not only calls us, but He also enables us, to become outrageously kind, unselfish, and humble men.

Trust Me

I remember watching the Indiana Jones trilogy as a young man. I—along with every guy I knew—was intrigued by this adventure-seeking, treasure-hunting archaeologist. His bravery was astounding, and his ability to persevere was always impressive. I can still picture him in each of the films with his hat pulled across one eye, a five o'clock shadow fully intact, and an intriguing half-smile, as he delivered the trademark line, "Trust me."

Apparently, however, Dr. Jones didn't expect those words to be taken seriously. He didn't prove himself to be the most trustworthy of men. He consistently placed others in dangerous situations, often lied to get his way, and broke at least three women's hearts in the course of his adventures.

It takes more than mere words to make a man trustworthy. As

we noted in chapter 3, a trustworthy person displays reliability and follow-through. A trustworthy person also demonstrates integrity and genuine care for the hearts of others.

Above all, a trustworthy man stands by his promises. He's a man of his word. He knows and obeys what Jesus said about this: "Simply let your 'Yes' be 'Yes' and your 'No,' 'No'; anything beyond this comes from the evil one" (Matthew 5:37).

A trustworthy man follows through with his promises. Consider the wedding vows. A man promises to love and protect his wife in sickness and in health. What if every time she became ill, he bolted for the golf course? If he cannot stand by his words, is this man worthy of her trust?

A trustworthy man also understands the power of his promises, so he's careful with his words. He recognizes that people will expect him to do what he says. Therefore, he chooses his statements cautiously and pledges only what he knows he can carry through. He remembers the scriptural promise that a man "who keeps his oath even when it hurts" will live with God forever (Psalm 15:4). He knows the Lord honors those who stand by their word.

A man inspires the confidence of others by being committed and responsible in all his relationships. Scripture makes it clear that this kind of man is worthy of trust and praise. He's a man who can be loved safely, for he will be faithful and true. He's also a man whose declarations of love can be taken seriously. A man may claim love, but without the actions to support his claim, his words ring empty and hollow.

"Many a man claims to have unfailing love, but a faithful man who can find?" (Proverbs 20:6). If you want to be worthy of trust, show your commitment to relationships. Follow through in love and reliability.

Finally, a trustworthy man fiercely guards the hearts of others. He is aware of how his words and actions affect others, so is careful to avoid hurting their feelings unnecessarily. Though he may make mistakes, the trustworthy man won't use or abuse the trust given to him. Eventually he proves that he can be trusted with someone's heart and that he's worthy of the ultimate trust of a wife.

A trustworthy man stands by his word, commits to his relationships, and protects the hearts of those who trust him. An outrageous man sets himself apart with kindness, unselfishness, and humility. And a holy man upholds righteousness, applies God's Word first to himself, and then leads others in the pursuit of godliness.

This kind of man is H.O.T. in every way and at all times. And unlike Mr. Bond, his hotness will last, for it has been built upon what is right, what is good, and what is real.

6

She's H.O.T.

From Jerusha

Cover Story

There are two ways to determine whether a woman is "hot." You either judge her by the standards of the world or you judge her by those of the Lord. In this chapter, we want to expose the views of the world for what they are—shallow, fickle, and immoral. Then we'll look more intently at what makes a woman H.O.T. in God's eyes.

The world plasters hot women on magazine covers, movie posters, CD labels, and even screen savers. You can't walk into any store without seeing some gorgeous girl promoting the latest product. If you wanted to, you could admire these women anywhere, anytime.

This superabundance of female images is said to be the result of a "guys like to look" mentality. Advertisers capitalize on the fact that men are typically more visual than women.

But marketing executives also know that men aren't the only ones looking. Women also look at women, but for completely different reasons than men do. Whereas the sight of a beautiful woman thrills men, the same image drives women to comparison and competition.

For many young women, the urge to compare and compete is subtle—so subtle that most would deny feeling jealous or unworthy. But actually, the media wants women to doubt their worth. They market "perfect" women in an effort to persuade girls to buy what they promote.

Magazines are some of the worst perpetrators of this manipulative marketing. Even though I know this is true, in the bookstore or grocery store I still find myself occasionally picking up the latest glossy-covered issue, intrigued by the headlined promises of articles like "How to Have Healthy, Happy Skin." The model smiles at me from the cover. I look at her pristine face, the clear, glowing skin. I know my own face well, and my skin doesn't always look "happy." At age twenty-three I still find zits.

Another article offers "50 Ways to Flatten Your Tummy before Summer." Of course the stunning blonde on the cover seems to have no need of this advice. Her tanned abs are taut and firm. In fact, her entire body manages to be tight and curvaceous all at the same time.

The headlines continue screaming: "How to Be the Hottest Lover Your Man Has Ever Had," "Our Astrologist Tells You What Month You'll Be on Fire," and "The Tell-All Quiz…Are You a

Dating Dud?" *Well, am I a dud?* I start asking myself. Quickly I flip to the quiz to reassure myself.

But wait. That's exactly what the magazine editors want me to do. They know I'll read because, like countless young women, I'm probably unsure of myself, unconvinced of my own worth. And they want me to believe *they* have the answers for all my life's questions. Their quizzes and articles and pictures promise to point me in the right direction. They want me (and you) to depend on them to settle the question of what's hot and what's not.

What those editors *don't* want you to be is confident of the real truth: that the blond babe on the cover has been plastic surgerized, fake-lipped, and tummy-tucked—and her photo air-brushed. That you don't need an astrologist to tell you when you're hot. That a twenty-question quiz can never determine whether you're worth dating or marrying. That the most fulfilling desire is not to be the hottest lover, but simply the *only* lover your husband will ever truly want and have.

Hollywood is as bad as the magazines at marketing hotness. Movie posters sport underdressed, undernourished women who are supposed to be our ideal of beauty and charisma.

And what about the films themselves? In high school I remember girlfriends saying they couldn't believe I hadn't seen *Pretty Woman*. They ranted and raved about how romantic it was or how they wished they could be Julia Roberts. So I watched it—and discovered that the heroine of this modern fairy tale is a hooker, selling her body for money. Is this really what women aspire to be? Is this what we consider romantic? Is a prostitute the kind of woman we want men to think of as hot?

I must admit the filmmakers did an excellent job portraying Pretty Woman's heart of gold. As a hopeless romantic myself, and a relatively undiscerning teen, I did find myself carried away by the movie as a whole. It did seem romantic and fun and lovely. But when I thought about it later, I realized it was just another airbrushed lie. What's really under the glossy, big-smiled facade is the immoral reality that this princess was a prostitute.

So where *can* a young woman turn for examples of what's truly hot? The music industry surely isn't the place. Recently I read a short article about a singer who shocked the public by wearing a very revealing "dress" (if you can call it that; it was more like a scarf) to the Grammy Awards. Some called her outfit the hottest thing on stage. She gloried in the attention, laughing about having to use tape to hold the dress up. To her, being hot translated into revealing as much as possible. Stars or not, such women don't have a vision for what's truly H.O.T.

Young women can't look to television either. TV is filled with subtle and not-so-subtle images of how women should look and act. Shows continually preach in a nonbiblical way about fashion, friendship, sexuality—every topic you can think of. Programs like *Extra* and *Entertainment Tonight,* for example, are often about appearance. They devote large amounts of airtime to the battle actresses fight with their weight.

What happens if that young singer who prides herself in flaunting her hot bod today gains weight? She may find herself the subject of a tabloid slam tomorrow. What torture it would be to feel that you're worth something only if your face and body stay hot. What a shallow basis for evaluating women.

And then there's the supermodel who may see herself as beautiful each time she's glossed over and made up. But how can she go home and feel secure when the next photographer might say she just doesn't have it anymore? What happens when she gets older and her looks aren't so hot anymore?

So what makes a truly H.O.T. woman? How does she differ from the world's visions we've identified? How can she express her unique femininity in a H.O.T. way?

To answer those questions, let's look at a few characteristics of God's ideals for a H.O.T. woman. These are by no means all-inclusive, but they will lay a strong foundation for determining what makes a woman truly H.O.T.

The Holy Woman

Holiness isn't a uniquely masculine or feminine quality, but because men and women are different in many ways and because God has called them to specific roles within the kingdom, it's important to focus on how certain aspects of holiness apply to women. (If you've never investigated God's design for womanhood and don't understand the unique roles God has planned for females, read the "Just for Girls, Just for Guys" section of *I Gave Dating a Chance*.)

The first characteristic of a holy woman is that she desires God. She's interested in the *things* of God; but more than that, she is drawn to and in love with the *person* of God. A holy woman hungers for God.

With the psalmist she can say, "As the deer pants for streams of water, so my soul pants for you, O God. My soul thirsts for God, for the living God. When can I go and meet with God?" (Psalm 42:1-2).

A holy woman is eager to grow in her relationship with the Lord and longs to spend time with Him. She longs to read His Word, to share it with others, and to worship Him, for she knows He deserves to be praised. And God is glorified in her longing.

Yet God isn't the only one who enjoys this yearning. This hunger and thirst are also fulfilling to her. She knows the truth of what Jesus says, "Blessed are those who hunger and thirst for righteousness, for they will be filled" (Matthew 5:6).

A holy woman's pursuit of God results in gratification. Jesus, the Living Water and Bread of Life, quenches the thirst and satisfies the hunger deep within her. Should she hunger and thirst for anything but Him, her longing would prove futile. Nothing but the One and Only God can satisfy the deepest cravings of the heart and soul. The woman who is satisfied with Him will desire Him all the more, and as a result, she will be filled to a deeper degree. This cycle of desire and fulfillment goes on and on.

As she knows God more, a holy woman begins to act and think righteously. This upright lifestyle, called "virtue," is the next key to being a holy woman.

Proverbs 31:10 asks, "Who can find a virtuous wife? For her worth is far above rubies" (NKJV). Women of virtue have always been few and far between, but the H.O.T. man knows her value and will settle for nothing less in a date or a wife.

The dictionary defines *virtuous* as "morally excellent; upright; chaste." Virtue is the conformity of one's life and conduct to moral and ethical principles. I would take it a step further and say that virtue is conformity of one's life and conduct to *the* moral and ethical principles—the standards of the true and living God.

The world's examples of the hottest women (we looked at a few) all lack true virtue. No moral excellence or uprightness can be seen. Chastity is a joke to them, and conforming their lives to anything except their own desires seems out of the question. No wonder the proverb asks, "Who can find a virtuous wife?" Moral rectitude and purity are rare and precious commodities.

Holy women are women who know God's principles and live by them. Holy women are physically and emotionally chaste, morally excellent in conduct, thought, and speech, and upright in all they do. They are women who choose to sanctify their lives in conformity to God's will. And they're worth more than this world's most precious jewels.

Therefore Christian women (along with male believers) are told, "Do not conform any longer to the pattern of this world, but be transformed, by the renewing of your mind. Then you will be able to test and approve what God's will is—his good, pleasing and perfect will" (Romans 12:2).

We will conform either to the world's pattern of a hot woman or to God's ideal. We can choose to pursue the superficial, capricious, and licentious, or we can choose to be women of virtue who hunger and thirst for God. If you choose the world, beware. That path will eventually lead to misery and death, whether from disease, abandonment, or just aging. The world's version of hot lasts only for a moment.

On the other hand, the path of virtue will lead to life-affirming wisdom and insight. The Lord promises that, by conforming to His standards, a woman will be transformed and able to determine His good, pleasing, and perfect will. Unlike anything the world offers, her transformed mind and character will last for all eternity.

The final characteristic of a holy woman relates to how she is transformed and how she conforms to God's principles. Yielding to the Spirit and seeking the guidance of more mature believers is key to her holiness. God's Spirit working within her does the bulk of the work, and sometimes the Spirit works through other people to sharpen and refine her in dynamic ways.

That's why a wise and holy woman who longs for God and demonstrates virtue also submits herself to mentoring by older women of faith. God established this pattern long ago, when He inspired these words in Scripture: "Likewise, teach the older women to be reverent in the way they live…to teach others what is good. Then they can train the younger women to love their husbands and children, to be self-controlled and pure, to be busy at home, to be kind, and to be subject to their husbands, so that no one will malign the word of God" (Titus 2:3-5).

Do you want to be the best possible girlfriend, fiancée, and wife? Then surround yourself with women who model love for their husbands and children. Do you desire self-control, purity, and kindness? Allow yourself to be led and guided by older women who have walked the path longer. Respect their experience and glean from their understanding.

As one of the many volunteer leaders for a large church youth group, I saw a prime example of how a Titus 2 relationship works. Erica, a girl who truly put the "holy" in "H.O.T.," was loved and respected by all. Busy with school and church activities, Erica had little spare time. She had many friends, both guys and girls, and could have easily spent every minute of her free time with them.

But Erica wanted more than just peer fellowship. She yearned to be closer to Jesus and to exemplify virtuous femininity. She longed to be guided by someone who knew what that meant. So instead of waiting around for an older woman to approach her, Erica showed great initiative by pursuing a mentor herself.

Erica sought out Molly, another volunteer staffer. Erica had observed Molly's character and knew she could learn a great deal from her. So she asked if they could meet once a week to talk, pray, and study together.

Molly and Erica sharpened each other, and their relationship became truly precious to both of them. Erica could have gone on just hoping she would someday enjoy this kind of one-on-one mentoring. But she didn't wait. She went after it, and God blessed her desire and motivation.

Pray that God will show you whom to ask to be your mentor. Don't let shyness or lack of time stop you. God will work out the details because He desires you to grow in virtue and in your love for Him. He wants you to have that quality guidance.

If the person you ask says no or flakes out after two meetings, that person simply isn't God's mentor for you right now. Keep praying that God will lead you to the right person to help you grow.

Holiness equals growth—and the holy woman is always pursuing a deeper walk with Christ.

Hear Me Roar

What does it mean to be an outrageous woman?

You might think of the attitude expressed in the song "I Am Woman, Hear Me Roar," which asserts a woman's right to complete independence and total control over her own life. The song has become a battle cry for die-hard activists who wish to eradicate all differences between the sexes.

To clarify, that group does not represent what some call the "feminist movement." Feminism started with women who wanted the right to vote. Feminists fought for equal pay for equal work and for freedom of opportunity for women. Traditional feminism didn't set out to destroy the precious uniqueness of the sexes.

But some activists have taken the idea of equality to an extreme. They claim that in order to be equal, they must shed their femininity—in a sense "become men." (As if starting as a woman and staying a woman isn't good enough!)

I don't know about you, but I have no desire to be a man. I love being a woman, and I'm happy about the differences between the genders. This statement rings true to me: "The more alike the sexes become, the less exciting relationships between them are bound to be."[1]

I was drawn to my husband because he was a man, different from me. He and I complement each other and fit together. I don't want him to be like me, and he doesn't wish I were more like him. He chose me in part because of the unique expression of femininity in my personality and appearance.

But there are those in our culture who would nullify both femininity and masculinity. They see feminine uniqueness as a threat and want everyone, male and female, to be the same. They see no personal value in developing the characteristics that make a woman feminine.

God does see value in male/female differences. He could have easily created a single gender. He could have made some "male" and others "more male." But instead, "God created man in his own image; in the image of God he created him; *male* and *female* he created them" (Genesis 1:27). God designed a world with two genders to complement and enhance one another.

That leads us to the first aspect of an outrageous woman: She develops and values her femininity. In today's society, a woman who respects, appreciates, and grows in her individual femininity is truly exceptional and noteworthy.

Now being feminine doesn't mean wearing lipstick or bows in your hair. It doesn't mean never getting dirty, or always matching your shoes with your belt. (You laugh, but I found out this was a huge priority for some of the women I went to college with in Texas.)

Being feminine has more to do with the way you think and act than it does with how you dress or what sports you play. Being feminine means being comfortable with your womanhood, not despairing of it.

God created all women with different combinations of feminine traits. A girl may not dress in skirts and lace, but still have a tender, motherly heart. On the other hand, the most "girly" dresser may be less emotional than some of her male friends.

The trick is to discover your own feminine qualities and develop those to God's glory. An outrageous woman knows she's different from all her friends. She looks for the distinctly feminine things in herself and accentuates them.

I'm the type of girl who loves wearing dresses, skirts, and an occasional bow in my hair. I don't shy away from lipstick. But I don't like to paint my nails, and I hate to shop. When I work out,

I like to sweat rather than keeping my hair in place and my makeup intact.

Sometimes my feminine qualities seem contradictory. In college, I played on a powder puff football team whose motto was "Kill, maim, destroy." At the same time, I'm extremely sensitive to violence in films and can't watch some movies even though I know they aren't real. I didn't do much baby-sitting in middle school, but I know I'll adore caring for my own children someday.

Every woman can work to make herself more feminine, even if you don't feel or think of yourself as feminine. There are two areas of improvement that I can pinpoint specifically.

The first is charm. "Oh no," you groan. If sickening visions of Victorian girls balancing textbooks on their heads and drinking tea come to your mind, then I say, "RELAX!"

Charm simply means the ability to please or attract through personality or beauty. I want to focus first on personality. To a large degree, charm is learned and developed. If you have worldly charm, you observe people's likes and dislikes and adjust accordingly. But to have godly charm challenges your personality to step up a notch.

When you take an interest in things outside yourself, you develop godly charm. Anyone can acquire this kind of charm. It only takes self-discipline, a regard for others, and the Holy Spirit working in you.

Yet charm proves to be somewhat elusive for many young women. They're simply too wrapped up in themselves to care about others. This kind of selfish woman is unable to make others around her comfortable.

Being near a charming woman is like being drawn into a magical place where everything is purer, brighter, and more tranquil and safe. A charming woman radiates care and concern, and that attracts others.

But a charming woman doesn't lose herself in the process of caring about others. On the contrary, she grows in individuality and intelligence while investing in the lives of those around her. To other women, she's a friend and confidante. To men, she's an encouragement, spurring them on to pursue their dreams and to be the best they can be.

To become an outrageously feminine woman, work on developing genuine interest in the lives of those around you. Others will be drawn magnetically to this kind of true charm.

Another aspect of charm that every woman can work at is her grooming. I hope I've been very clear that the way a young woman looks or dresses doesn't make or break her femininity. But some Christian women don't care properly for their appearance and justify that choice with the "spiritual" line "I don't want to focus on external beauty."

Every woman ought to take pride in her God-given appearance. Good grooming is attractive; bad grooming repulses people. Sloppiness is not next to godliness, even if you're making a concerted effort to focus on your heart and soul rather than your face and figure. Ask yourself, "Do you not know that your body is a temple of the Holy Spirit?" (1 Corinthians 6:19). God wants us to care for all parts of His temple.

As I was enrolling at Rice University in Houston, I heard that the school had the ugliest women on any American campus. Rice chicks supposedly focused on the brain and forgot about the rest.

What began as a slam eventually became a source of school pride. I saw women who prided themselves on their sloppy appearance. In their sweat shorts and gnarled hair styles, they laughed about the "Rice image." But then they wondered why they never had dates. They didn't connect their slovenly appearance with the way they were viewed and treated.

Part of being uniquely feminine is looking different from a man. You can do this in a variety of ways. Maybe it's as simple as a pair of feminine shoes or earrings. Maybe it's wearing your hair in a more feminine style or putting on lip gloss. Discover what feminine grooming works for you and take pride in doing it well. Realize that your grooming will express your femininity in a way that differs from every other woman's.

An outrageous woman is comfortable with her femininity on all levels, including her appearance. She takes care of every part of her body, knowing it is God's temple.

That leads me to another characteristic of an outrageous woman: She knows her own worth. She's not only feminine, she's also confident.

We read in Proverbs 31:25 that a woman of noble character "is clothed with strength and dignity; she can laugh at the days to come." She doesn't agonize over the future and is confident enough not to worry about it. She carries herself with dignity and self-respect, and her strength cloaks her heart with confidence. This woman knows who she is and enjoys it!

In *The Feminine Journey,* Cynthia and Robert Hicks point out that "women have never enjoyed more opportunities for freedom, yet they do not seem to be experiencing the inner peace and contentment they expected would accompany this liberation."[2] The world tells women that the more opportunities and success they have, the more confident they will be. But this doesn't prove true over the long haul. Women with many worldly accomplishments aren't necessarily happier than those with none or few. Society encourages women to develop their individuality and independence, but peace and confidence don't necessarily follow.

True, each woman must develop her unique individuality. She must learn to appreciate who God made her to be and the things He's gifted her to do. But this appreciation is the *result* of confidence, not the key to it.

Genuine confidence comes from knowing you're worth something, not that you've earned or achieved something. Many women make the mistake of assuming that their worth comes from some career position or degree or award. But God calls women to recognize that their worth stems from the fact that He paid everything—so that they might dwell with Him in love forever. Jesus gave up life itself that we might enjoy freedom in Him and life eternal with Him. No woman could be worth more, and no woman is worth less.

An outrageous woman knows that the question of her worth was answered for good when Jesus Christ died on the cross. Before they crucified Him, the Lord could have decided, "Jerusha really isn't worth *dying* for!" Praise Him, He didn't. He paid the price to buy my worth. He paid the same price for every woman. No greater evidence of a woman's worth is possible or necessary!

Knowing her worth in the Lord's eyes, an outrageous woman is confidently able to accept love and attention in appropriate ways. Some young women have trouble allowing themselves to be complimented and appreciated. They consistently reject the very attention that their insecure hearts crave. Whenever someone tries to express admiration or thanks, they're quick to shove it aside.

This systematic avoidance is called "discounting." Everyone knows what it means to discount something. Discounting reduces its value. In the same way, a woman who discounts loving attentiveness reduces her own value. She's basically saying, "I don't believe I'm worthy of what you're saying." She's also implying that the giver of the compliment isn't telling the truth.

Discounters may see themselves as undeserving of attention or praise. Others may falsely see themselves as humble and selfless. But while selflessness and humility are virtues, discounting is not. It destroys relationships because it reduces the value of both the giver and receiver of the compliment.

An outrageous woman is one whose sense of worth is secured in the price Jesus paid to love her. She can laugh at the days to come, she's clothed in self-respect, and she can accept the thanks and love of those who wish to honor her.

Now I haven't been particularly good at believing in my worth and developing my own confidence. I have struggled for many years feeling inadequate and insecure about anything and everything. But I'm growing in this area, and I want to continue to grow. I want to be able to laugh at the days to come, trusting that my worth depends not on my accomplishments, but on my trust in the God who gave up everything for me. If you, like me, have battled with insecurity and anxiety, please don't despair. God will work in you each and every day, as you allow Him to. He will make you more and more confident—more and more outrageous—as you surrender your life to Him.

One more characteristic of an outrageous woman is that she lives in the now. She obeys Christ's words in Matthew 6:34—"Do not worry about tomorrow, for tomorrow will worry about itself. Each day has enough trouble of its own." How true that is! Whenever I find myself worrying about the future—tomorrow, next month, or next year—I'm brought back to the reality that today holds enough for me to face.

The truly outrageous woman focuses on the present and on what God is calling her to do with it. This applies particularly to single women desiring a boyfriend or husband. The outrageous woman doesn't pine away for a man, but uses her singleness as a time to deepen her relationships with the Lord and with others while she becomes someone even more worth knowing.

Gladys Hunt puts it this way: "If a woman spends her time dreaming only of what could be…she ceases to live in the *now.* And no one is attracted to an empty shell. You don't start living when a man comes into your life; you have to live *now.* You have to be someone worth knowing if life is to be rich."[3]

The outrageous woman lives in the present, looking for ways to make the now the best that it can be. She doesn't find validation for herself in a man, but busies herself finding out what God would have her be and do as an individual.

Femininity, confidence, and living in the now are three outrageous qualities that make a woman remarkable and extraordinary. They set her apart and cause others to take note of her.

The Trustworthy Woman

Male bashing has become a popular pastime, making its way into movies, books, and even our homes. In the movie *Jerry Maguire,* I remember a scene showing a group of dissatisfied females. Their claws were out, and these catty women began blaming all the men in their lives for this or that. I admit, some of their gripes were funny.

What's not funny, however, is that male bashing has become just as prevalent among Christians as among nonbelievers. But it's really nothing more than thinly veiled gossip.

Gossip is any idle talk about the private affairs or character of another person. A statement doesn't have to be a rumor or an untruth to be gossip.

Many women excel at male bashing as well as at old-fashioned rumor-mongering. You'd be hard pressed to find a group of men sitting around gossiping about their friends or enemies. To find such a group of women, however, you need not look too hard.

In sharp contrast, a trustworthy woman doesn't gossip—and this may be the most important quality of a trustworthy woman. She knows when to hold her tongue and how to speak about others in a way that brings good, not harm. H.O.T. women take seriously the biblical charge to tame their tongues: "Do not let any unwholesome talk come out of your mouths, but only what is helpful for building others up according to their needs, that it may benefit those who listen" (Ephesians 4:29).

If you're talking about someone, consider before you speak whether your words would help or hinder that person and whether they would build up or tear down the listener. And consider how untrustworthy you appear when chatting idly about the intimacies of another person. A trustworthy woman doesn't engage in loose talk.

Another characteristic of a trustworthy woman is that she's quick to listen. She knows the wisdom of this verse: "Everyone should be quick to listen, slow to speak and slow to become angry" (James 1:19).

You may be unaware of—and surprised by—how men view

the listening skills of women. A study of over fifteen hundred marriages revealed that men's number-one complaint about their wives
was that their wives talked too much and listened too little. One
restaurant in California made light of this by taking the name *The
Quiet Woman;* the sign out front displayed a woman with no head.

I honestly had no clue that men felt this way. When I read
about the study, I ran in to where my husband was watching *The
Crocodile Hunter* or some other manly show. I begged him to tell
me that I wasn't such an awful listener. He said I wasn't, but I wonder if that had more to do with the fact that he wanted to get back
to the crocodiles.

Since making this discovery about men's perceptions, I've
become much more aware of my listening skills. I've found that
sometimes I really am a very poor listener. And I thought about
what that communicates to my husband.

First of all, it makes him feel that what he's saying isn't worth
my time or energy. But what's more heart-wrenching is realizing
that it makes him unable to trust me. How could he fully trust
someone who doesn't listen carefully to him? So, as a woman who
desires her husband's trust, I'm trying to use my senses in better
proportion—since, as the old saying goes, God gave us two ears
and only one mouth.

Listening shows that you're more interested in the other person than in yourself. Saint Francis of Assisi prayed these words
which may inspire you: "Grant that I may seek not so much to be

understood as to understand; to be loved as to love." If this prayer reflects the desire of your heart, your listening skills will grow exponentially.

I encourage you to develop the skill of listening now. Make it clear that you're a woman who can be trusted with the ideas, beliefs, and feelings of others. A trustworthy woman protects the heart of her friends, her dates, and eventually her husband. When others tell you about themselves, never use those words against them.

A trustworthy woman avoids gossip, listens well, and protects the heart of others. An outrageous woman is feminine and confident, and she lives in the now. And a holy woman is one who hungers and thirsts for God, who models virtue, and who allows herself to be mentored by mature women of faith. Those characteristics together make for one truly H.O.T. woman!

How H.O.T. Are You?

Jerusha's Story

In high school, I did my fair share of dating. I enjoyed going to school dances and other functions, and I spent my weekends with groups of friends or on dates. I really wasn't interested in a serious relationship with any of the guys, so my involvement with them remained casual and short.

After I graduated, my parents confessed that they couldn't understand what I saw in some of the guys I dated; they were so different from me. They were right about that. Since having fun was my only goal in dating, I hadn't thought much about the whole process. I wasn't terribly selective about who I went out with. And though I professed faith in Jesus as my number-one priority, I didn't always choose guys who shared that commitment.

As I entered college, I consciously decided that I would change my approach to relationships. But my early college days proved no different from high school. I just went out and had fun, never considering what the consequences might be.

This dating without thinking had negative repercussions in my life. Many times the young men I dated wanted to pursue a more serious relationship. Since I was just "having fun," I ended up hurting their feelings and losing some friends.

I also hurt myself. In my freshman year of college, I became deeply attached to a guy who didn't share my faith. Though I knew cutting ties with him was right, it pained me greatly to do so.

The worst consequence of my not thinking about dating was that I damaged my relationship with the Lord. More and more distance grew between Him and me as I dated those who didn't spur me on to holiness, outrageousness, and trustworthiness.

During my second year of college, I recommitted my life to Christ in areas where I realized I had slowly taken control. One of those areas was dating. As God opened my eyes to what I had been doing, I felt ashamed and regretful.

Looking back, I wish I had learned earlier to make wise choices about dating. I wish I had decided ahead of time what type of guys I should and would date. Not only would I have avoided hurting others, I also would have avoided grieving my Lord.

Over a period of time, Jesus changed my life in some powerful ways. He showed me sins that I hadn't even imagined were issues. One of these areas was my relationships with guys, and what I realized about myself hit me so hard that I felt I was back at square one.

At the same time I recommitted those areas to Christ, I began meeting with a volunteer staff member from one of the Christian organizations on campus. We got together to discuss biblical issues, to talk about what was happening in our lives, and to share prayer requests.

The Lord used Ruth to help me see many things about myself that I either didn't want to see or couldn't see on my own. And it wasn't easy. There were many tense moments and even some tears during those meetings.

You see, at first I wasn't very teachable. I didn't really want her to mentor me. In fact, I thought that I could handle pretty much anything. I acted as if she had nothing to share with me that I didn't already know or couldn't find out on my own. What a bonehead I was!

But gradually Ruth helped me to see I needed others to walk beside me in the life of faith. During both my second and third years of college, we kept meeting, and she knew most of what was happening to me. I shared with her some of my frustrations about dating and relationships, and she listened patiently. She often offered advice, and she always prayed for me when I asked her to.

Once I was telling her about how I always seemed to attract guys that didn't fit the description of what God wanted for me. Ruth said she felt she understood what caused the problem—and I was all ears.

"Jerusha," she continued, "before you can find someone worth finding, *you* must first become someone worth being found."

Let me say that another way: In order to find someone H.O.T., you must first be someone worth finding. Before you can find someone who's H.O.T., you need to work on being holy, outrageous, and trustworthy yourself.

It had never occurred to me that *I* was the problem. I'd never imagined that I wasn't attracting the "right" kinds of guys because I wasn't the right kind of girl. I had never dreamed I needed to work on myself.

The words on a greeting card I later received emphasized this point: "Marriage is not so much finding the right person as it is being the right person." Let me take that truth one step further: *All* relationships, whether friendship, dating, engagement, or marriage, are not so much about finding the right person as being the right person.

If this idea rocks your world as it did mine, don't worry. Recognizing your need is the first step toward change. Once you're open to this truth, God will be at work in and through you to make you a totally H.O.T. guy or girl.

After Ruth shocked me with her statement, I started researching what it was God wanted *from* me, not just what God wanted *for* me. I began turning my life over to Him more completely.

The results were phenomenal. My friendships and dating relationships improved dramatically. I became more aware of how and what I communicated to others and more focused on building relationships in which trust remained in Christ and intentions were clear. As I became a woman worth being found, I learned to date to God's glory.

Just by reading this book, you're already so far ahead of where I was that day when Ruth's words got my attention. In the previous chapters you've seen not only what God wants *for* you, but also what He wants *from* you. Now let's focus on that even more, as we look at a few strategies for improving your H.O.T. qualities.

I Can't Get No...

Imagine a world in which everyone was satisfied. No one would complain about how loudly you played your music or how you dressed or how well you did or didn't do your work. No one would suffer from road rage. Drive-by shootings and car-jacking rates would hit record lows. Come to think of it, crime would practically disappear.

But let's get back to reality. Humans tend to be a pretty dissatisfied bunch, wouldn't you agree? No kid ever gets enough bubble gum or ice cream. No girl ever thinks she's pretty enough. No guy ever feels he drives the perfect car or makes enough money.

And how many young adults can say they've found true satisfaction? From the conversations I've heard, I'd say not many. Most of the time, young adults downplay their strengths and focus on their weaknesses. They dwell on their own flaws or the flaws of others. They often express feeling empty and unfulfilled.

So what's the alternative? Get H.O.T.! And one of the best ways to get started on the path to becoming H.O.T. is to learn that true satisfaction comes from Christ alone. Only He can completely fulfill you. If you aren't content in the Lord, you'll never be satisfied with another person.

Sometimes we reverse things and first try to find satisfaction in relationships with others. Those of us who do this quickly discover how miserably this strategy fails. We usually end up feeling either that we're not good enough for others or that others aren't good enough for us. Either way, we can't find satisfaction in other people.

Bottom line: Get your significance and satisfaction from Christ Jesus.

Have you ever read Shel Silverstein's book *The Missing Piece*? This short story chronicles the tale of a circle who's missing a pie-shaped wedge that would make him complete. He searches high and low for his missing piece, believing that he'll obtain true happiness and satisfaction only when he locates it.

He finds some pieces that look as if they might fit. He tries them out, but they're too short or too fat or too loose. In vain he tries forcing them in, desperately wanting to fill the void that keeps him feeling incomplete.

All of us human beings resemble that incomplete figure. We've been created with what philosophers call a "God-shaped void" in our hearts and souls. No piece on earth will fill that space. We may try, as the circle did, to force various things to fit. Some people attempt to fill that void with money, success, or good deeds. Some try worse things—alcohol, drugs, or other addictions.

But the most common "piece" that people try to make fit is other people. We try to use friendships, especially romantic relationships, to complete us and make us whole. But other people can never entirely fulfill us.

God created us with an emptiness that only He can fill because He wants us to yearn and long for Him. He wants to show us how perfectly He can and will complete us. He wants us to be able to pray sincerely, "Earth has nothing I desire besides you. My flesh and my heart may fail, but God is the strength of my heart and my portion forever" (Psalm 73:25-26).

The Lord designed us to be lonely without Him. He created us to be incomplete and dissatisfied when we aren't finding our fulfillment in Him. This is why so many of us, even those who belong to Him, experience discontentment and frustration. We're trying to fill our God-shaped loneliness with things other than Him.

But we need not fear the loneliness, the dissatisfaction, or the lack of fulfillment that comes with simply being human. You see, God created that void within us to draw us closer to Him. Therefore, the first step on the road to being H.O.T. is learning to be satisfied and content with Jesus. He alone can fill the greatest missing piece in your life.

As He does, then you will more and more be able to say with Paul that you have "learned the secret of being content in any and every situation, whether well fed or hungry, whether living in plenty or in want" (Philippians 4:12). The key to that secret is this: "Don't fret or worry. Instead of worrying, pray.... Before you know it, a sense of God's wholeness, everything coming together for good, will come and settle you down. It's wonderful what happens when Christ displaces worry at the center of your life" (Philippians 4:6-7, *The Message*).

Allow Christ to replace all the dissatisfaction and discontentment in your heart. Let Him meet your needs and grant your desires. Let His wholeness work everything out for your good.

Paul knew that genuine contentment comes when you focus on who you are in Christ. So learn to focus on the fullness, the perfect completion that is yours in Jesus. By doing this, you will grow in the H.O.T. qualities and open the door to healthier relationships with others. You'll expect less of them because you know from the outset that they can never fill the God-shaped void in your heart.

Under the Microscope

The ancient philosopher Socrates proclaimed, "The unexamined life is not worth living." Thousands of years later, his words remain true. Life cannot be worthwhile without introspection and personal growth.

As Christians, we should examine our lives in light of God's Word. We should allow its perfect truth to guide and shape us to be more like the Savior we love. We should continuously evaluate our lives because we desire to mature in Him.

In fact, the second step on the path to becoming H.O.T. involves such a spiritual checkup. The reality is, the more time you spend looking for Mr. or Mrs. Right, the less time you have to make sure that you're becoming Mr. or Mrs. Right yourself. So slow down for a moment and take some time to examine your own life. Allow God to reveal what He desires to change in you.

Not only will this self-examination improve your relationship with Him, it will also improve your personality. As General Douglas MacArthur once noted, "Life is a lively process of becoming...if you are [always] thinking the same thoughts having the same predictable reactions, rigor mortis of the personality has set in."

Are you suffering from rigor mortis? Have you become too predictable and unchanging? Do you spend more time looking at other people than working on yourself? Perhaps it's time to take inventory of what's inside your own heart.

In 1 Corinthians 7:32-34 we find the standards by which a single man and woman should take spiritual inventory: The single man, Paul writes, "is concerned about the Lord's affairs—how he can please the Lord." Paul says the same is true for a single woman. She "is concerned about the Lord's affairs: Her aim is to be devoted to the Lord in both body and spirit."

In examining your life, would you say that you're concerned with the Lord's affairs? Do you even know what His affairs are?

One of the primary ways to show concern for God's affairs is by fixing your mind on Him, which is a result of living by God's Holy Spirit. "Those who live according to the sinful nature have their minds set on what that nature desires; but those who live in accordance with the Spirit have their minds set on what the Spirit desires" (Romans 8:5). If you're concerned with the Lord's affairs, your thoughts will reflect it. Your mind will be fixed on what the Spirit desires.

What Do Your Friends Think of You?

We've already covered a lot in this book. As you have read about what it means to be H.O.T., have you found yourself responding, (a) "Yeah, that's me" or (b) "I've got a lot to work on"?

If your answer is (b), take heart. You're on the right track. As you continue to grow, you'll find yourself becoming more like the H.O.T. person we've described. Get started with the first two steps we've talked about: finding satisfaction in Christ and living an examined life.

The third step toward becoming H.O.T. is to discover what others see in you. We can all benefit from the counsel of older and more mature Christians who know us best. So take some time to sit down with an older believer who knows you well. Run through the different H.O.T. qualities and ask this person to evaluate your strengths and weaknesses in each area.

If you need some help getting started, here are some questions to ask your friend...

Holy:
- How do you see my personal walk with God?
- How do you view my public walk with God?

Outrageous:

- What are the strengths and weaknesses of my personality?
- What are my remarkable or unique qualities?
- How well do I demonstrate joy? How well do I encourage joy in others?

Trustworthy:

- Am I a reliable person?
- How would you rate my authenticity and honesty?
- Am I protective with the emotions—the hearts—of others?

For Guys:

- Am I growing in Christlike leadership?
- Do you see me as a person who follows through with my commitments?

For Girls:

- How do I demonstrate virtue and where do I lack it?
- Do I express confidence in who I am?

You may not feel comfortable asking someone these exact questions, so feel free to create your own questions based on what you've read in this book. You may want to write down your questions, then ask someone you respect and trust to write their responses in detail, offering you any guidance or advice. Be sure to follow up after you've received this input. Not only can you thank your friend, but you can also ask for further information to clear up any misunderstandings or confusion. Remember, your goal is to get the most accurate representation possible of what this person sees in you. That way you'll know what areas of growth you need to pursue.

It may be difficult to face some of the things that others see in you. But you will benefit greatly from their wisdom if you open yourself up to learn from them, and as you remember that to find someone H.O.T., you must first become a holy, outrageous, and trustworthy person yourself.

H.O.T. Talk

Don't Play with Matches

One morning last week, we awoke to the distinct smell of fire. Naturally this concerned us. We walked outside, scanning the horizon for signs of smoke, hoping not to see flames. Nothing. No black billows, no red glows.

Later we learned from a news report that a wildfire raging hundreds of miles away had caused the smell. The blaze had consumed thousands of acres and forced the evacuation of hundreds of people. Firefighters battled valiantly, but it would be many days before the wildfire was contained.

And what started this huge mess? A match? A jumpy flame from someone's barbecue grill? A curling iron left on or a stove unattended? No, this fire had been started on purpose. Meant to be a "controlled fire," the blaze became a monster of annihilation and misery. One insignificant bit of fire got away and sparked a raging, unmanageable horror.

How often does the spark of one uncontrolled word or misdirected comment start a wildfire in your life?

Imagine arriving at school on a Monday morning only to have your best friend practically attack you in the parking lot with these words: "Ohmygosh, you won't believe what they're saying about you!"

The infamous "they"! The "they" who start rumors that fly around with the same destructive force as a forest fire. The "they" who can destroy your reputation in moments. The "they" who seem to thrive on false accusations that keep smoldering for months or years.

What if the rumor concerned you and another person and your purity was called into question? What you supposedly did after the dance Friday night has suddenly become the hot topic for everyone at school. "They" analyze your relationship and pick it apart, and new details get added each time the rumor is repeated.

Wild talk can devastate just as easily as a wildfire can.

Or have you ever had a conversation with a guy or girl whose words wounded you so deeply that you felt your heart had been scalded? Maybe you were breaking up. Maybe someone uttered a sarcastic comment as you were passing in the halls. The painful words stay with you, don't they? You replay them in your mind, wondering if they're true and wishing they had never been spoken.

Words can scorch and sear, leaving the ashes to linger in your heart.

Few of us fully appreciate the power of words in relationships, and words spoken in the context of guy-girl interactions have a unique and immense force. For some reason, we seem to take more seriously the words spoken by someone of the opposite sex, especially someone we may be interested in. We hang on their every syllable, dissecting their possible intentions and trying to figure out what they truly mean.

What If...

Can you repeat verbatim some painful words spoken to you in the past? Almost all of us nurse deep wounds that words have inflicted on our hearts and minds. Words like *ugly, fat,* and *stupid* may not literally break our bones, but they can be imprinted on our minds and engraved on our hearts.

"It only takes a spark, remember, to set off a forest fire," the Bible tells us. "A careless or wrongly placed word out of your mouth can do that. By our speech we can ruin the world, turn harmony to chaos, throw mud on a reputation, send the whole world up in smoke and go up in smoke with it, smoke right from the pit of hell" (James 3:5-6, *The Message*).

Does that word picture help you understand the intense power of your words? Catch these passages, too: "The tongue has the power of life and death, and those who love it will eat its fruit" and "He who guards his lips guards his life, but he who speaks rashly will come to ruin" (Proverbs 18:21, 13:3). Wrapped up in our very words are life and death, our prosperity or our destruction.

We've all been victims as well as the perpetrators of painful words. As James says, "If you could find someone whose speech was perfectly true, you'd have a perfect person, in perfect control of life" (James 3:2, *The Message*).

As a person who wants to be H.O.T. and to enjoy a relationship with someone else who's H.O.T., never forget the power of your words. And realize especially that words spoken between a man and woman are almost an entirely different language—a language of the heart. You feel in your innermost being the wonderful weight of those three simple words "I love you." But the weight of the words "I never want to see you again" can crush your very soul.

As a H.O.T. person, be constantly aware of what you're communicating. Choose carefully what to talk about and what to avoid. Learn to steer every conversation to the glory of God.

Seldom Is Heard...

We've focused mostly on the negative power of words, but the same force can be used in a positive way, honoring God and blessing others.

That's why we should strive to use our words to build others up. A H.O.T. person knows how to encourage.

That word *encourage* means to inspire with confidence, spirit, or courage. In the New Testament, the Greek word translated as "encourage" comes from a root word meaning "to build"; the Greeks used a form of the word to describe a person who constructs houses.

Through encouragement, you build up the "house" of some-one's heart and spirit. You help them see in themselves something positive they may have overlooked or undervalued.

Encouragement imparts hope, confidence, and enables people to persevere. As Chuck Swindoll once commented, "We live by encouragement and die without it. Slowly, sadly, and angrily."

The Lord commands each and every one of us to encourage others. "Therefore encourage one another and build each other up" (1 Thessalonians 5:11). Since we all need it, we should all be busy encouraging others.

Wouldn't it be wonderful if life were like the wide-open plains that cowboys croon about in "Home on the Range," where "seldom is heard a discouraging word"? Too often, in our schools, our homes, and even our churches it is the *en*couraging word that is seldom heard.

One major way that a H.O.T. person can set himself or herself apart is through learning and practicing the art of encouragement. You can comfort a hurting friend or simply make someone's day a little easier by offering the kind of words spoken about in Proverbs 16:24: "Pleasant words are a honeycomb, sweet to the soul and healing to the bones."

(*From Jeramy:* You can do this with both spoken and written words. Nearly every day, Jerusha slips a note in my lunch. The few sentences of love and encouragement she writes sometimes change the course of my day.)

As we experience trials, encouraging words from others allow us to move forward in hope. Recently we went through some difficult times when negative comments seemed to come at us from every direction, and we felt unappreciated and unloved. We were able to offer each other life-saving support and love through encouraging words.

Don't underestimate the power of encouragement in a relationship. Learn to encourage your brothers and sisters in Christ. This is definitely a quality that separates the H.O.T. from the not.

Slipping Lips

William Norris, a nineteenth-century novelist, offers this advice:

> If your lips would keep from slips,
> Five things observe with care:
> To whom you speak
> Of whom you speak,
> And how, and when, and where.

A H.O.T. person recognizes the wisdom of this rhyme and learns to be aware of every aspect of his or her speech.

Interactions between guys and girls call for a special awareness of what certain words or subjects may communicate. For example, if the homecoming dance is just around the corner and a guy keeps bringing it up with one girl in particular, chances are she'll think he's planning to ask her to be his date. If that is not his intention, his loose lips and lack of awareness could end up hurting her feelings.

Looking again at those lines from William Norris, we see that the first aspect of avoiding lip-slips is an awareness of "to whom you speak." If you know a certain person has shown an interest in you, you want to be more careful about what your words to that person might connote. In other words, know your audience.

Knowing if a person is sensitive about certain subjects or to specific types of jokes will help you avoid saying things that might cause pain or misunderstanding.

People who are H.O.T. always know their audience. They adjust their speech to best serve the person they're talking with; they don't speak without thinking. They know that not everyone receives comments or ideas the same way.

The next part of keeping your lips from slips is knowing "of whom you speak." Conversations about other people usually end up being more trouble than they're worth. Statements can so easily be misinterpreted or taken out of context. Imagine you spoke to a friend about being interested in getting to know someone else. Next thing you know, it's practically on the network news that you like that person. Now your chances of getting to know him or her in a stress-free atmosphere are almost nil.

A H.O.T. person always remains sensitive to what he or she says about others and leaves their private business unspoken.

The last three aspects in Norris's lines—"how, and when, and where"—are also essential to keeping your lips from slips.

Be aware of your inflection and intonation. Sarcasm can come in with just a slight change in the tone of your voice. Consider how your words will fall on the ears of others. You may think your intentions were clear, but your tone of voice or even your facial expression can communicate something just the opposite.

Also, bear in mind that when and where you say something may make a difference. Nighttime is definitely a more serious and romantic time than broad daylight. So midnight under the moonlight may not be the best time to tell someone who's just a friend, "I'd really like to see you again." In that setting, those words can suggest something more than you intend. The same goes with talking about kissing late on New Year's Eve or Valentine's Day.

Look for and become someone who thinks seriously about how your speech reflects your intentions and personality. Look for and become a person who uses words to honor others. Look for and become a holy, outrageous, and trustworthy person who is set apart by knowing what to talk about and what to avoid.

Sometimes Silence Really Is Golden

You can probably remember a few times when you wish you had simply held your tongue—when silence would have kept things "golden."

It's not always a negative comment that destroys the peace. Some of the kindest words spoken can cause the deepest hurts if they lead someone to assume more than they should. That's why H.O.T. people know when to hold their tongues.

A H.O.T. person prays with David, "Set a guard over my mouth, O LORD; keep watch over the door of my lips" (Psalm 141:3). Ask the Lord to help you stay silent when you need to be. Pray that He would help you find a H.O.T. guy or girl who knows how to do the same, that you might encourage each other to hold your tongue in the right moments.

Proverbs 17:27-28 says it all: "A man of knowledge uses words with restraint, and a man of understanding is even-tempered. Even a fool is thought wise if he keeps silent, and discerning if he holds his tongue."

Bottom line: All of us probably need to talk less. One of our shared "life verses" as a couple is this one: "When many words are present, sin is not absent" (Proverbs 10:19). The more you talk, the more opportunities your tongue has to spark a forest fire.

Work at developing the skill of silence, and look for another who will encourage you in this endeavor by his or her example. A truly H.O.T. person doesn't have to talk all the time, but knows when it's best to hold his or her tongue.

The Right Stage

H.O.T. people also recognize that different kinds of relationships demand different levels of communication. A H.O.T. person's words are appropriate for whatever stage the relationship is at, and they don't force emotional intimacy too quickly. They are words that help set and maintain boundaries that guard the heart.

In his book *Why Am I Afraid to Tell You Who I Am?* John Powell identifies five basic stages of communication.[1]

The first is the kind of small talk you might have with someone in an elevator or on a bus. You speak about neutral topics like the weather and reveal little if anything of yourself. This first stage is reserved primarily for strangers; you share almost nothing because you have no idea if that person can be trusted with that knowledge.

Revealing facts is the second stage of communication. At this point you're willing to reveal things about yourself such as where you work, what sports you play, or what hobbies you enjoy. These facts require no investment of opinion. You share nothing that could be readily disagreed with or rejected. This may be the level of communication when you've just met someone at a party, for instance. You're testing whether to proceed to stage three of communication—the sharing of ideas and opinions.

In this third stage, communication becomes a bit trickier. You must be willing to risk opposition or even exclusion if you express an opinion that could offend or upset the other person.

After determining that the other person is both interested in what you have to say and willing to accept it even if he disagrees, you may move on to the fourth stage of communication, the revealing of emotions. This is more dangerous ground, because the rejection of one's emotions is more painful than the rejection of opinions. Emotions are below the surface, coming from our hearts, so they are more closely tied to who we really are.

The final stage of communication is transparency. Many people never even approach this stage because of the high level of risk it entails. Transparency is complete openness, the full sharing of the "real you" from the heart. Transparency requires a great deal of trust and a secure level of commitment. Transparency equals emotional intimacy. You share deep joys, fears, hopes, dreams, and sorrows with each other.

Now imagine meeting someone for the first time. You start talking about what kind of activities you each enjoy, what kind of pets you have, what sort of music you like, and how many brothers and sisters you have.

Then suddenly this person starts bawling and confessing (between sobs) something about having never had a pet canary and having to go through years of therapy to heal the psychological scarring from being deprived in this way. You get a little freaked out at this point. And rightly so!

This person shared something that wasn't appropriate for the level of your relationship. It's one thing to share a deep hurt with someone whom you've known and loved, but to jump all at once from stage two to stage five can cause problems.

Now that example may be extreme, but we want you to get the point: Keep your level of communication appropriate to the stage of your relationship!

A H.O.T. person knows that revealing deep emotions may

cause someone to assume a level of intimacy that really isn't there. H.O.T. people also know that to guard their hearts they must reserve transparency for those who can be trusted completely.

Too often, we've seen young people try to jump into the transparency level in a relationship without realizing that later, if and when the two of them break up, a piece of their heart will be taken.

So look for people who guard their own heart, for they will guard yours as well. Authentically H.O.T. people will not push you to an improper stage of communication. They will be aware, just as you are, that the level of the relationship should define the level of communication.

Friends communicate on a different level than engaged couples do. Husbands and wives communicate on a different level than engaged couples do. This is right and good. It reserves the best, most intimate parts of you for the person with whom you'll spend the rest of your life.

As your relationship progresses through the stages of friendship, dating, engagement, and ultimately marriage, make sure that you keep your communication appropriate.

H.O.T. Walk

A Day in the Life...

When the alarm announced that 6 A.M. had arrived, seventeen-year-old Brian Ashton hit the snooze button and rolled over on his left side. Fifteen minutes later, the beep, beep, beep roused him only long enough for him to smack the snooze again. Finally, two snooze-smacks later, Brian wearily dragged himself out of bed.

The warm haze of sleep still hung on him as he brushed his teeth. After a shower, he picked his clothes out a little more carefully than usual. After all, this was Wednesday, and he always liked to look his best for youth group on Wednesday nights.

Brian downed a bowl of Cinnamon Toast Crunch and reached for his keys hanging by the door to the garage. "Oh no," he groaned. He'd forgotten to take the trash cans to the corner last night for the regular Wednesday morning pickup. He rushed back through the kitchen and out the back door, grabbed both bulky containers at once, and rolled them around the house and out to the edge of the driveway. He jogged back into the garage and jumped into his Mazda B2000 pickup.

Turning the ignition, Brian felt good. He said a quick prayer thanking God for reminding him about the trash. He hated seeing the disappointed look on his mom's face every time he forgot.

The ten-minute drive to school always flew by. This morning he thought about the day ahead. No tests, only a few weeks of school left, and the junior prom this coming weekend. A fine day, he decided.

He parked as close as he could to the spaces reserved for seniors, knowing that in a few months one of those coveted spots would be his. He glanced at his watch. 7:07.

Brian headed for room 218, the counseling office where his first-period class would meet. Called peer assistance, it was set up for students to drop in and share their struggles with someone their own age.

Brian had signed up for a leadership spot in the program after his youth pastor challenged their group to find a way to serve on their school campuses. Brian enjoyed the class tremendously, and his advisor observed that he had a real gift for helping others talk through their problems. This class always made Brian feel good.

This Wednesday no students came by to talk, so Brian spent the forty-five-minute period catching up on the history reading he hadn't done last week, and which he was supposed to be able to discuss in class next hour. When the bell rang, he slammed his textbook shut and took off for the social science wing.

Taking his seat, Brian noticed other students with their books open, madly flipping through the chapter he'd just read. His eyes roamed the classroom, looking for the explanation. He found it on the blackboard: "Pop Quiz Today. Take out a pen and blank piece of paper."

As Brian pulled out the pen and paper, he thanked God for giving him the last period to read. He also asked God to help him remember what he'd just read. When the bell rang to start class, Brian felt confident and peaceful.

A few hours later when his lunch period arrived, Brian grabbed a slice of pizza and a Pepsi, looking around the lunchroom to find his friends. He saw them packed around one of the circular tables and wondered if he could squeeze in. He hated having to stand or sit alone.

When he got to the table, everyone was laughing at something Trevor had just said. Brian tapped Melody on the shoulder and asked her to scoot over. He had chosen to bother Mel because she was the most kindhearted of the group. A real sweetie.

But for some reason, Mel was being difficult today. "Uh, sorry," she said in an uppity tone. "There's no room."

Brian felt his face turning red. He couldn't just slink away after being shut down by the sweetest girl he knew. The words fell out of his mouth before he could stop them: "Well...maybe that's because your big hair is taking up too much space."

Everyone let out a collective "Oooh..." Brian realized he had "won." They all knew that moving here from Arkansas two years ago hadn't cured Melody's affinity for big hair.

Then he caught Mel's eye. She looked like she had been slapped. He saw a tear. She rose as quietly as possible, grabbed her drink, and mumbled something about needing to get to class early. In a flash, she was gone.

No one else at the table missed a beat. Everyone went on talking and laughing about the coming prom or last night's episode of *ER*. Brian gingerly sat down in Mel's seat. Trevor slapped him on the back and laughed at his "joke" about Mel. But Brian felt sick and barely touched his pizza.

Halfway through fifth period, he started thinking about how to apologize. Algebra II wasn't his favorite subject anyway, but today he found it impossible to concentrate.

Mel would be in his sixth hour class, physics, and in fifteen minutes he'd have to face her. "Lord," he prayed silently. "I'm so sorry I said that to her. Help her forgive me. And help me keep my mouth shut. Thanks."

Brian felt better.

Sixth hour came, and Melody was as gracious as she usually was. She must have seen that his apology was genuine, which it was, and she showed no interest in giving him a hard time. She laughed it off and gave him a quick hug.

Just outside the door to the physics lab, Brian felt someone pull his arm. It was Grant, who lived down the street from Brian and had been his best friend growing up. But after Brian made a commitment to Christ in his freshman year, their lives sort of went in separate directions. Grant had stayed with the party crowd while Brian formed new friendships. Still, Grant always included Brian in whatever schemes he had cooking.

Today he wanted to talk about an after-prom kegger. One set of parents in the party crowd always managed to be out of town on prom weekend, and this year would be no exception. "At the Reynoldses'," Grant said to him in a mock whisper. Brian knew the house—definitely a classy place.

Grant's eyes were huge as he described their plans. Brian started wondering what he'd missed out on by avoiding those kinds of parties. He fell into deep thought and barely heard Grant's parting words.

He made it to the gym a split second before the seventh-hour tardy bell. In the locker room, he dressed out slowly, still thinking about the kegger. He knew what temptations he'd face there and honestly didn't think he could handle them. That's why, after giving his heart to Jesus, he'd eventually made a commitment not to go to any more parties with alcohol.

He did a slow jog out to the track and started his laps. Two of his old buddies, Ryan and Greg, caught up with him on the second loop.

"Hey, dude," Greg panted. "Did Grant tell you about Saturday?"

"Yeah," Brian answered.

"You gonna bring Shelley?" Ryan asked, nudging him in the ribs and nodding strangely.

Brian looked over at him but didn't answer.

"Dude," Ryan went on, "it's like the make-out palace. You're sure to get her there." Ryan and Greg laughed. Brian felt like stopping and knocking the stupid grins off their faces.

Shelley was one of the prettiest girls in school. For months Brian had wanted to ask her to the prom. He had built up the courage only a week ago after learning that she still didn't have a date. She had turned down a couple of guys who had questionable reputations. Brian knew it had to be because of her standards as a Christian.

"We've already got plans for after prom," Brian told his two buddies. With that, he took off sprinting, finishing the mile well ahead of most of the class. He raced through the stretches and circuit training and had already showered before some of the guys made it into the locker room. A few minutes later the bell rang, and he was free.

After school he did homework and ate a quick dinner. He made it to church just in time for the 5:30 youth group leadership meeting. Brian's team organized and ran the group's Friday night coffee house. For this Friday, they were planning a mock game show and music from a local songwriter.

Leadership team spilled over into youth group. After a warm-up game and a worship time, the youth pastor, Eric, taught a lesson that really caught Brian's attention. Eric spoke on how to revitalize a lagging devotional life. For weeks now, it seemed that Brian rarely had a spare minute for devotions. And when he did have a quiet time, it was dry.

Eric told the students that feeling distant from God occasionally was normal. He asked if they ever felt distant from their parents or their friends. *Sure,* Brian thought.

"Your relationship with God will go through the same kind of ups and downs," Eric assured them. "But God never moves and He never changes, and if you keep going to Him through the dry times, the 'valley' times, you'll feel His presence again before you know it."

That night as Brian crawled into bed, he pulled his Bible off the nightstand and opened to Proverbs because Eric had recommended reading one chapter of this book each day. He spent some moments in prayer, thanking God for a great day, and then turned out the light at 10:30—making sure the alarm was set for tomorrow morning, and the beginning of another day.

W.A.L.K.

You may wonder why we would go to such great lengths to describe a day in the life of Brian Ashton. Well, we wanted you to focus with us on what it's like for a believer to walk with Christ through an average day. Obviously Brian isn't perfect, but it's clear his life belongs to the Lord. He's walking with God.

If you want to become a person worth being found, learn to

walk with Christ. And any H.O.T. person you might want to date or marry should have an active and dynamic walk with Jesus too.

You've no doubt heard the phrase "walking with Christ" often enough. But what does it mean? Are you supposed to take a stroll in the park every day, pretending you're holding Jesus' hand?

No. Walking with Christ means much more. We've broken it down into four components, which you can remember with the acronym W.A.L.K.—*W*orking for the Lord, *A*lways turning to Him, *L*iving in purity, and *K*nowing His Word.

Walking with Christ basically means that your love for and desire to serve the Lord determine every aspect of your life. Your life belongs to Him.

Working for the Lord

"Whatever you do," we read in Colossians 3:23, "work at it with all your heart, as working for the Lord, not for men...."

No matter what you do, you can make every task a service to the Lord. Brian served in several ways throughout his day. He took the trash out, which was a service to both his family and his God. It was a simple act that took only a minute or two. Sometimes we have the perception that offering assistance or doing something extra will eat up our entire life if we let it. But many acts of service are simple and take very little time. And the rewards for them far outweigh the sacrifices.

Brian also signed up for peer counseling and found out that, in serving others, he was blessed as well. He felt as uplifted by the time he spent counseling others as the people he served did. This shatters another misperception about service—that it's really all about "others." Serving others is one of the ways God uses to bless us. And He uses it to change us as well, to make us less self-centered and more like Christ. When you're serving, you tend not to think about your own desires and needs.

In *Celebration of Discipline*, Richard Foster writes, "Nothing disciplines the inordinate desires of the flesh like service."[1] Service takes your mind off yourself and puts it on God and His will. When you're in that state, the Lord can speak to you and use you.

But what about working for the Lord in other ways? Did you notice how Brian committed his history quiz to the Lord? You can even work for the Lord in school by asking Him to be glorified in your studies. Remember, you're not just working for men (or grades or getting into college), but for God Himself.

Always Turning to Him

Another aspect of walking with Christ is committing every step and every decision to Him—everything. A person who truly walks with Jesus refers everything to the Lord, from huge life decisions to minute-by-minute choices.

Most of us Christians take the "big deal" stuff to God. If we have to choose a college or decide whether to go on a summer mission trip, we'll pray about the choice. When we have a terrible day, we run to the Lord and pray for mercy, hope, or healing. But we often fail to go to God with the little things. We fail to acknowledge Him on the days when things are going just fine.

Oswald Chambers said this: "We need to rely on…Jesus much deeper down than we do, to get into the habit of steadily referring everything back to Him; instead of this we make our common sense decisions and ask God to bless them."[2]

Walking with Jesus means inviting Him to be part of your day—your *whole* day. This is a sign, Chambers says, of true discipleship, of an intimate knowledge of Jesus Christ that nothing can shake.

You can become intimate with someone only by spending time with that person. Are you walking with Christ closely enough that you refer everything back to Him? Are you a true and intimate disciple?

God doesn't always use the huge things to show Himself clearly. In fact, His miracles don't make Him seem as special or as near as His many small blessings do. It's usually in the "little things" that the Lord reveals how intimately involved He is with us.

Brian walked with the Lord by always turning to Him and referring things to Him. He thanked God for the small blessings: a reminder to take out the trash and the chance to catch up on his reading before a pop quiz. He also prayed for the Lord's help on that quiz, showing that he knew God cares about the details of his life. Finally, when he made a hurtful comment to Mel, he felt convicted by the Holy Spirit. This showed that he's close enough to the

Lord to feel remorse and to desire repentance. Brian prayed for forgiveness and sought to make things right with his friend. Finally, he ended his night with thankful prayer.

As you can see, turning to God has much to do with prayer. "Of all the spiritual disciplines," Foster says, "prayer is the most central because it ushers us into perpetual communion with the Father."[3]

Isn't that the point of turning to God in all things—to be in communion with Him, to be close to Him? Prayer will help you stay tightly knit to God. It also allows you immediate access to His throne. He will hear your prayers anytime, anywhere, whether you're in history class or kneeling beside your bed.

Another part of turning to God is acknowledging Him in every circumstance. Brian could have considered it "luck" that he remembered to take out the trash, but he *chose* to acknowledge God. He could have credited "fate" for his having time to study during first hour, but once again he appreciated God instead. And he could have easily shrugged off the hurt Mel experienced because of his comment. His friends all laughed, so why should he feel bad? But Brian realized that God's standards were higher than his or those of his friends.

Brian was experiencing the powerful truth of this promise in Scripture: "Trust in the LORD with all your heart and lean not on your own understanding; in all your ways acknowledge him, and he will make your paths straight" (Proverbs 3:5-6). Brian chose again and again to see how God was in control. And he was blessed because of it: He knew he wouldn't be in trouble about the trash; he took the quiz with confidence; Mel forgave him graciously; and, at the end of the day, he was sincerely thankful for God's guidance, direction, and love.

By always turning to God in prayer and acknowledging His sovereignty, a person can walk more closely with the Lord.

Living in Purity

Living in purity is another major element of walking with Christ. Jesus is completely holy and pure. He is the light. A person walking with Him will live in that purity and light.

If we lead impure lives while pretending to walk with Jesus, then we're nothing better than liars: "If we claim to have fellowship with him yet walk in darkness, we lie and do not live by the truth" (1 John 1:6). To walk with Christ in purity implies that confronting anything dark and impure draws you closer to the light—closer to Jesus Himself.

Brian was confronted with darkness in the form of an invitation to a kegger and an opportunity to speak vulgarly and disrespectfully about his friend Shelley. These instances drew Brian back to the truth, back to the light. Seeing the pitiful things the darkness had to offer, he made choices based on his commitment to purity and goodness.

And notice that he didn't have to make a huge statement to Ryan and Greg. All Brian had to do was say no and walk away.

Sometimes living in purity simply means standing firm and letting your actions speak for themselves.

As Oswald Chambers defines it, *purity* means "unsullied walking with the feet, unsullied talking with the tongue, unsullied thinking with the mind—every detail of life under the scrutiny of God. Holiness is not only what God gives me, but what I manifest that God has given me."[4]

To "sully" means to mar the purity or luster of something. To be unsullied, then, means to remain pure and untarnished. We challenge you to be unsullied in your emotions and thoughts. We challenge you to remain pure physically, in speech and in action. And we challenge you to stay pure practically, in everything you do.

Purity shows itself in a number of emotional, physical, and practical ways. Brian showed emotional purity by recognizing his guilt in hurting Melody's feelings. An impure person wouldn't have given it a second thought. He also demonstrated emotional purity by declining to go to the kegger. He may have been tempted, but he chose to do the right thing.

He showed physical purity by refusing to be part of his friends' conversation about Shelley. He wouldn't let his tongue speak impurely. His response to Ryan and Greg implied that he was also committed to physical boundaries—the "make-out palace" wasn't somewhere he would let himself go.

Finally, Brian showed practical purity—putting yourself in the right places and taking yourself out of the wrong ones—by simply walking away from the temptation to indulge in further improper conversation with Ryan and Greg. He just got out of there.

Living in purity involves engaging your heart, soul, mind, and strength in making wise choices according to God's standards. Brian's life demonstrated a commitment to purity on several different levels. As a believer who desires to please the Lord, your life should reflect a similar devotion to staying pure in speech, thought, and action.

Knowing God's Word

This last aspect of walking with Christ may be the most essential. God reveals Himself to us in His Word, and unless we know it, we cannot truly know Him.

Jerry Bridges nails this on the head: "Walking with God involves communion with God. His Word is absolutely necessary and central to our communion with Him.... It's impossible to practice godliness without a constant, consistent, and balanced intake of the Word of God in our lives."[5]

Wow! It truly is *impossible* to practice godliness—or to walk with Christ—without knowing God's Word. Immersing yourself in the Word of God is profitable and necessary if you desire to walk with Him.

Of the many verses about knowing and loving God's Word, one of our favorites is this one: "I lift up my hands to your commands, which I love..." (Psalm 119:48). Throughout this psalm we find a myriad of reasons why we should love God's Word. His

Word gives us light (verse 105), freedom (verses 32 and 45), understanding (verse 130), and peace (verse 165).

The psalmist makes God's Word a priority in his life: "I meditate on your precepts and consider your ways. I delight in your decrees; *I will not neglect your word*" (119:15-16). We wish that everyone would pray that prayer! When people are asked how much they read their Bibles, the all-too-common answer is "not enough." Most of us neglect God's Word at some time or another.

Brian showed a desire to know God's Word. He went to youth group and listened intently to the teaching. Corporate or group learning is an essential part of knowing God's Word. That's one of the main reasons to go to church.

Brian also spent solitary time at home in the Word of God. His plan to read one chapter of Proverbs a day is a great one. This book offers chunks small enough to bite off, but big enough to chew on.

Once you begin to read and know God's Word, you will become hungrier and hungrier for it. Before long, one proverb or psalm won't be enough to satisfy you. You will crave more time in the Word because through it you learn more about your Lord, your Savior, and your Friend.

Both public and private time in the Word is essential for Christians who long to walk with Christ. As you grow in your knowledge of God's Word, the other aspects of walking with Him will deepen as well. Because Jesus sets the best example of service, you will desire to serve others as He did. You will also have more to pray about, and you will more readily turn to God first. And as your mind is filled with His thoughts, you will desire more purity and light in your life. Nothing but good comes from knowing God's Word.

Grown Up

From now on, when you hear the phrase "walking with Christ," we hope you think of *W*orking for the Lord, *A*lways turning to Him, *L*iving in purity, and *K*nowing God's Word. As you walk with Christ in these ways, you'll become "mature and complete, not lacking anything" (James 1:4). You'll grow up in the Lord.

"What does it mean to be grown up?" Chuck Swindoll asks. "It means having the self-discipline and commitment of an authentic walk with Christ seven days a week; the determination to obey God and to submit to the truth of His Word at any cost; the ability to nourish myself as an individual believer in God's Word; the compassion to reach out and care for other people whose needs are different from my own; the willingness to share in the responsibilities of the household [and doing] all of the above with an attitude of a contagious, positive spirit."[6]

May we all walk with Christ and grow up in this very way.

H.O.T. Meets H.O.T.

Now What?

Many young Christians know what they should look for in a dating partner. In past years they've heard teaching on the subject at church, and now they're ready to find a holy, outrageous, and trustworthy man or woman to date and ultimately marry.

But you may be surprised how many of these "I know what I want" Christians don't have the first clue what to do when they actually meet the H.O.T. person of their dreams. How *do* you develop a relationship with a H.O.T. person?

If you haven't the faintest idea, this chapter's for you. We'll dive into the practical side of starting and advancing a relationship in godly, healthy ways. We'll also look at how to take a relationship through the stages of friendship, dating, engagement, and finally into marriage.

Love Story

Over the past couple of years, we had the rare privilege of watching a precious and God-honoring relationship develop. Alex and

Kaitlyn have worked on the youth staff at our church since we came to Colorado in the fall of 1998. Back then they were "just friends." But recently we were blessed to witness and celebrate their marriage.

Alex and Kaitlyn have been tremendous role models to the young people at our church, and we want to share their story with you as an example of how two H.O.T. people proceeded through the stages of their relationship.

The two of them met the first week of Kaitlyn's college career. It was WOW week at their university, seven fun-filled days of crazy games, get-to-know-you events, and late nights. They were introduced to each other by Lori, another student at the college. Lori wanted the two of them to get acquainted as soon as possible. Somehow, she just knew they'd hit it off.

As she dragged Kaitlyn over to introduce her to Alex, Lori told her that she was about to meet her future husband. Kaitlyn laughed it off, but was intrigued by Lori's confidence.

When she first laid eyes on Alex, Kaitlyn thought Lori couldn't have been more wrong. It wasn't just that he had egg and whipped cream all over him from the last wild game. Other things about Alex took Kaitlyn by surprise—things like his shaved legs and painted toenails.

Granted, there were reasons for these things. Because Alex raced bikes, he shaved his legs to lower wind resistance. And junior high students had painted his toenails the night before in a scavenger hunt—though Kaitlyn wondered why Alex hadn't tried nail polish remover.

Though it was hardly love at first sight, Kaitlyn and Alex became fast friends as they pursued the common interests they shared, such as swing dancing and spending time outdoors. Each one noticed that the other was outrageous—fun, full of life, and remarkable in many ways. In the group activities they joined in together, they made certain no one could interpret the time they spent together as dates. Their friends wanted just to have fun as a group and not to "couple off"—and this was fine with Alex and Kaitlyn. They both thought the time wasn't right to invest in a romantic relationship, with each other or anyone else.

Over the next few months, Alex and Kaitlyn continued to develop their friendship, and Kaitlyn soon joined Alex as a volunteer leader in our church's youth group. The two of them would make the hourlong commute each week, which afforded them plenty of time to talk and laugh. They also saw each other in the context of ministry, which Kaitlyn vows is the best way to truly get to know someone. They appreciated each other's commitment to holiness and desire to serve God.

By Thanksgiving, they each admitted to themselves that they had feelings for the other. Still not sharing those feelings, however, they started praying about their relationship, asking God to direct them appropriately. One night soon afterward, they sat down together and told each other what they'd been feeling.

Alex and Kaitlyn were excited to discover that their feelings were mutual. At this point, they knew each other well enough to trust each other. Both had proven themselves to be reliable, full of integrity, and protective of the other's heart. Even so, instead of jumping into a romantic relationship right away, they chose to wait. They wanted to be sure they weren't making a decision based only on emotions. They continued praying about their relationship, and they began asking others for advice and guidance.

After Christmas break, they both felt God was confirming to them that dating was the logical and healthy next step, and they discussed this together. H.O.T. had met H.O.T.

A few days later they took us to lunch and told us of their decision to start dating. They asked us how our own dating relationship had progressed, and we spent the next two hours talking. We were impressed by their commitment to develop a healthy dating relationship. They wanted our support, and we were thrilled to give it.

For the next five months, Alex and Kaitlyn focused their dates on getting to know each other better and centering their relationship in Christ. They still went dancing with the gang, but now they were always partners. Both on and off the dance floor, they had fun discovering how they complemented each other in many ways.

The biggest change in their relationship at this stage was the increase in the amount of time they spent alone. There were many late nights of sharing ice cream and being absorbed in talking with each other. They talked about how to stay focused on what was real and true in their relationship—such as their commitment and what they knew about each other—rather than on feelings that ebb and flow.

As they spent more time alone with each other, they found it increasingly important to guard their hearts. They recognized that spending time together leads to deep and meaningful bonding. They always saturated their relationship in prayer and kept it accountable to friends and mentors.

Almost half a year passed before they experienced their first kiss. They had waited because they wanted their first kiss to represent a special and serious step in their relationship. Beginning a physical relationship called them to set up a new level of boundaries, and they were more cautious about the time they spent together late at night and alone.

As the months went by, they gave more serious thought to their future together. They knew God had blessed their relationship immensely. It seemed to them that the next appropriate step was engagement. Following the advice of Alex's parents, they began pre-engagement counseling with a pastor.

This counseling brought them face to face with some difficult realities. Yet through it all they realized they truly loved each other and wanted to spend the rest of their lives together.

Alex and Kaitlyn continued praying about their relationship and seeking the counsel of others. A wise friend told them that if they were praying, if others were praying for them, and if there seemed to be a consensus on what they should do next—then that was probably how God was leading them. God desires to show His will to us just as much as we want to know it. In this case, He blessed Alex and Kaitlyn's decision to take their relationship to the next stage.

On New Year's Eve, a year after they started dating and confident that God had led them and would continue to lead them in their relationship, Alex asked Kaitlyn to be his bride.

Their seven-month engagement was not a picture-perfect fairy tale. There was the pressure of planning countless wedding details with their families. There were tough times when their physical boundaries became harder to keep. And there were even some fights between these two who loved each other so much.

Through all these trials, Alex and Kaitlyn kept their eyes fixed on Jesus and their hearts open and teachable. They sought and then heeded the wisdom of more mature men and women of faith. They chose to kiss only now and then, knowing that as their wedding day approached, it would be more difficult to stay pure. And they treated their parents with respect and dignity, while holding fast to what they felt God calling them to do.

Now, throughout their life together as husband and wife, Alex and Kaitlyn will always have a story to tell of God's provision when they weren't looking for it, of God's blessing when they sought His will, and of God's wonderful gift of a H.O.T. person to love and marry.

We're Just Friends...

Alex and Kaitlyn developed their relationship in a careful, healthy, and godly manner. Their relationship progressed slowly, and they were always aware of where they were emotionally and what they were doing. They didn't deny their feelings, but kept them appropriate for each stage of their relationship.

They built a strong foundation of friendship before they ever went out on a one-on-one date. They participated in group activities with school and church friends, giving them plenty of opportunities to discover which hobbies and interests they shared.

After all, common interests help form the foundation for good friendships. Within the context of a shared pastime, you can learn much about a person. For Alex and Kaitlyn, working at church was one of the best ways to get to know each other. There they observed each other's heart for the Lord and devotion to service.

Conversations are also important at the friendship stage. They allow you to determine whether the two of you share similar ideas and goals. By talking together, Alex and Kaitlyn discovered they both wanted to go into full-time ministry and that their views of life were complementary in many ways.

As a friendship like this progresses, attraction may develop—usually as a mixture of physical and emotional attraction. A combination of the unique things about a person make you want to spend more time together and get to know this friend even better.

Many times, this attraction grows gradually rather than hitting you "at first sight." A recent conversation with one of the juniors in our youth group reminded us of this truth. She explained she hadn't been instantly attracted to most of the young men she found interesting and handsome. Only in getting to know their holy, outrageous, and trustworthy qualities did she find herself wanting to deepen the relationship.

This desire to spend more time with someone you're drawn to often leads to the next stage of relationship—dating. A date is simply a prearranged social engagement. A dating relationship begins when a couple decides to spend more and more social times together.

Going to the prom or grabbing coffee together are certainly dates, but you can enjoy these in a friendly, lighthearted way without having a romantic relationship. If your intentions are clear to the other person, you can remain at the friendship stage and keep romance out of the picture.

But once you've determined that you'd like to invest more in a relationship with a certain H.O.T. person, you may choose to define your relationship as a romantic one. Whichever way you choose to date—as friends or romantically—think through how you will act and speak. Set and maintain boundaries that are appropriate for the stage of your relationship.

The Dating Thing

In a dating relationship, two people purpose to get to know each other better in a variety of situations and circumstances. To do this in a healthy and God-honoring way, the couple may begin to spend time with each other's family, getting to know how the person interacts with loved ones. They may get involved in ministry together so they can observe each other's commitment to service. And as they spend time talking and sharing their lives, they should carefully guard themselves from inappropriate emotional or physical intimacy.

As Alex and Kaitlyn did, couples committed to appropriate dating relationships will talk about physical and emotional boundaries before the moment comes when they might be tempted to transgress those bounds.

If you don't know how to establish emotional and physical boundaries, please read chapters 9 through 11 in *I Gave Dating a Chance*. These chapters detail the importance of setting and maintaining boundaries to protect your emotional and physical purity.

A dating relationship can be wonderful, but it can also be dangerous. Like Alex and Kaitlyn, healthy daters continually check their priorities and boundaries and stay within the emotional and physical limits that keep their hearts pure and clean. Any intimacy—physical or emotional—is meant to lead to something much more serious. Once you've started down a road, it's extremely hard to go back.

It's also essential to ask older, more mature believers to help you keep your relationship pure by holding you accountable, as Alex and Kaitlyn did. Relationships that are healthy remain aboveboard and answerable to others.

A healthy and godly dating relationship progresses slowly and cautiously. The couple plans their dates, letting the Bible guide their decisions about what to do and what to keep away from. They plan to honor God on each of their dates and in all of their conversations. Because they've set emotional and physical boundaries, they know what they will and will not do and say. This type of dating relationship is thoughtful, prudent, and free—free from harmful and sinful elements.

A final note about dating: Some H.O.T. young men and women have chosen to abstain from dating. While there's nothing wrong with this standard, there is something wrong with forcing it on others.

If you've been criticized for being open to dating, don't despair. We wrote *I Gave Dating a Chance* to answer the question "Can young believers date and honor the Lord at the same time?" Both in our own lives and in the experiences of people like Alex and Kaitlyn, we've found that the answer is yes.

As you form your own convictions about whether or not to date, consider these wise words from Oswald Chambers: "You have to walk in the light of the vision that has been given to you and not compare yourself with others or judge them; that is between you and God."[1]

Will You Marry Me?

At some point in a dating relationship, a couple may decide they can't imagine spending the rest of their lives without the other person.

Even knowing this, however, it may not be easy for the couple to proceed to the next level—engagement. Engagement can be a scary prospect. You've probably heard of couples who date for years on end while friends tease them that they should just tie the knot and get it over with.

(From Jeramy) Fortunately for us, I didn't let the fear of engagement stop me from popping the question. Jerusha and I had arrived at a point in our relationship where we knew we loved each other. We hadn't said the words "I love you" yet, but the feelings were definitely there. We just didn't want to speak that phrase to anyone except the person we *knew* we were to marry.

One Monday morning I was having breakfast with my mentor and friend, Doug Haag. Doug was asking me a number of questions about my relationship with Jerusha. I'd been hesitant to move our relationship forward, but that morning I began to see that engagement was the natural next step.

Finally Doug issued the challenge: "Jeramy, what are you waiting for?" He helped me see that it was time to make my move.

Spurred on by Doug's encouragement, I planned an amazing proposal, which culminated on gorgeous Catalina Island. In a botanical garden overlooking the Pacific Ocean, Jerusha and I promised ourselves to each other.

At that moment, the wild ride of engagement began. I remember feeling overwhelmed as, only minutes after I'd proposed, Jerusha began to spout off ideas for the wedding. I felt like saying, "Slow down! It took me a lot just to get to this point!"

But we couldn't stop the frightening speed at which wedding plans overtook us. There were so many little decisions to make, and every friend and relative seemed to have an opinion about them—some good, others ridiculous. Sometimes we'd just laugh or scream together about the intensity of it all.

But we didn't know the meaning of *intense* until we started premarital counseling. Wow! Talk about some tough times. After going through counseling with three different mentors, we earnestly believe that premarital counseling will either make your relationship or break it.

During our sessions, many issues arose that we had no idea were beneath the surface. Family history, different ways of coping, and even our assumptions about each other boiled up and over, causing some of our relationship's hardest moments.

Once we had to return for an emergency session because the counselor was afraid we would call the whole thing off. Yes, premarital counseling was tough.

But what we learned through it was priceless. We learned first of all that love is a choice. You may not always "feel the feelings," but if you've made the commitment to love each other, you can and will persevere.

We also learned that there are no perfect matches. Before counseling, we considered ourselves just about as perfect a couple as you could find. After counseling, we realized we had to work through and deal with a myriad of imperfections. We praise God we didn't break it off because we were afraid of such conflict.

For some couples, however, breaking the engagement is the only solution. Rachel's story made this clear to us. Rachel started dating Kenny in high school, and their romance was the first for each of them. Neither of them were believers in Christ at the time, and their physical and emotional boundaries were loose.

After graduating from high school, Rachel committed her life to Jesus. She and Kenny were engaged at this point, but Kenny didn't share her desire to serve the Lord. In fact, he refused to respect her new boundaries and pushed her to the point of despair and tears many times.

Rachel finally broke off the engagement, though it was the most difficult thing she'd ever done. For her, splitting up truly was the best option, and she trusted God to take care of the details.

Fortunately for us, our common love for each other and for the Lord helped us weather the storms of engagement. In fact, in the very midst of these difficult times, we discovered some wonderful things about our relationship.

First we realized the depth of our dedication to each other. If any friends or family members tried to come between us, we defended and stuck by each other. What a marvel it was to see someone you love choosing to give your relationship priority over and above all others.

We also learned that when we said, "I love you," we meant those words with all our hearts. We trusted each other so much that we expressed feelings and dreams we would never have shared with others. The deepening of our emotional bonds made our conversations all the more marvelous. We felt closer and more in love with each passing day.

And we were able to express that love in a different way as now we added a new element to our relationship—kissing. We had decided not to kiss until we were engaged, a standard that proved difficult to maintain many times while we were dating. Once we were engaged, we relished the first kiss and each one afterward.

As your own relationship with someone H.O.T. moves into the engagement stage, it's important to realize that there will be tough times. But engagement is also a precious time of exploring the new depths of your relationship. You can marvel at each other's loving commitment, enjoy the deeper conversations that allow you a more revealing look at your spouse-to-be, and delight in a pure and healthy physical expression of your love.

Two Are Better Than One

Engagement leads to the final (and best!) stage of a relationship—marriage.

Marriage begins with one of the greatest days of your life, your wedding day. Friends and family gather to celebrate, anxiously awaiting the hour when the two of you will be joined before the Lord. We cannot count the number of times we have looked back on our fairy-tale wedding and taken great joy in the memories. We picture in our minds the dance floor at our reception, crowded with the glowing faces of friends and family members who had supported and loved us through the years. Those memories remind us that we aren't alone in this marriage.

A couple of friends we know were given the opportunity to use $20,000 either to make a down payment on a home or to pay for their wedding. They chose the wedding, and we wholeheartedly agree with their choice. Of course your wedding doesn't have to cost $20,000 or even $5,000 to be wonderful. But having some kind of celebration in which your dearest loved ones witness your commitment makes for the strongest start a marriage can have.

Even after the wedding, the wonders of marriage are greater than any dream or fantasy. Sharing your life with another person is the most precious gift God can give you. Because of the safety and security of marriage, you no longer have to be guarded with your most vulnerable thoughts, secrets, dreams, desires, or fears. You know that you can trust your husband or wife to love you through anything.

The intimacy a married couple shares both emotionally and physically honors God and expresses love to each other. In the short time we've been married, we've found ourselves living out the scriptural principle that, in marriage, two become one (Genesis 2:24, Mark 10:8). We've begun to think, act, speak, and dream alike, and we look forward to growing even closer as God continues His refining work in our marriage.

In ministry, we've seen how much better we are as a team than we were on our own. We complement and stretch each other. As a couple, we accomplish more, love others better, and are more balanced than we were as individuals. It's the truth of Ecclesiastes 4:9—"Two are better than one, because they have a good return for their work."

Marriage is the ultimate stage of a male/female relationship, but that fact doesn't mean that your relationship stops growing and changing. The two of us have so far to go in the areas of communication, love, and patience—to name a few. And we are thrilled that we get to do it together, with the precious intimacy of oneness and the commitment to love and cherish each other by God's grace and power.

But marriage may be a long way off for you—so don't look too far ahead. As you develop your relationships, remember that the best stage you can be in is the one you're in now. If you're just friends, then dreaming about marriage with that person won't be beneficial. Develop your relationship with awareness and caution, just as Alex and Kaitlyn did. Enjoy and make the most of every relationship. Then when H.O.T. meets H.O.T., you'll know it and be prepared to pursue that God-honoring relationship.

Real H.O.T.

No Compromise

Our good friend Aaron is a youth minister who has devoted himself to the Lord's service—and he enjoys a "no compromise" kind of life.

Aaron strives for the best in all areas. We've observed his continual laboring to improve his youth group. We've noticed his wise financial stewardship as he's successfully invested in a home and in stocks. And we've also had the privilege of encouraging Aaron to remain committed to high standards in his relationships, while maintaining the utmost respect and concern for others.

Aaron is an attractive man who has had many opportunities to date, but he just hasn't felt ready to "drop the rock." He's holding out for someone altogether holy, outrageous, and trustworthy.

Since he's already twenty-six, some people ask why he doesn't just find a nice girl and settle down. But we know the truth. Aaron resists the temptation to go with the flow and to "settle" for someone who may not be God's best for him. Sometimes he's accused of being too picky. But there's a difference between being picky and being selective. Someone who's picky focuses on nonessentials, while a selective person recognizes that settling for anything less than God's best would be a compromise. Holding on to high standards for a holy, outrageous, and trustworthy date and mate is commendable, but sometimes tough. There's always the temptation to compromise.

Working in youth ministry, we've seen many who, unlike Aaron, allow their standards to drop. They've given in to peer pressure or to their own loneliness. They've failed to keep their standards high and have settled for a relationship with someone who's less than H.O.T.

Take Emily's story, for example. A lovely young woman, Emily attracted many guys—some H.O.T., some not. Her fun-loving, free-spirited attitude tended to draw guys who weren't committed to the Lord's standards.

The compromise in Emily's life didn't happen overnight. Like all temptations to settle, things started small: She accepted a date from a Christian who wasn't really "on fire" for the Lord. Then it was a guy who knew the truth but had walked away from the faith. Finally, it seemed perfectly okay to date whomever, whenever. As long as her own faith remained intact, Emily reasoned, dating these guys would be all right.

But it wasn't all right. Emily's faith didn't remain strong. Hanging out with guys who didn't pursue a relationship with God affected her ability to love and serve the Lord. Little compromises in her relationships led to compromises in other areas of her life as well. She was slipping, but so slowly that she didn't recognize it—until suddenly she feared she was too far from God to go back.

But Emily did go back. Fortunately, she hadn't committed to spending her life with someone who wasn't God's best for her. She admits she made many mistakes in dating. But she did turn back to the Father. As she surrenders her past failures, God will guide her into healthy, God-honoring relationships with men.

Others aren't as fortunate as Emily. Some step much further into compromise by marrying a man or woman who isn't H.O.T. Later they find that it's almost impossible for a H.O.T. Christian to share a fulfilling life with someone who isn't also holy, outrageous, and trustworthy.

Liz has discovered that truth. She wishes she had been more careful while she was dating Mike, the man who's now her husband. Mike never professed to be a believer, but Liz thought he was close to giving his life to Christ. Throughout their dating relationship, they talked about spiritual things, went to church together, and seemed to share a common vision.

Everything changed after Liz and Mike said their vows. Mike stopped going to church altogether and began saying things like "I don't want to have anything to do with *your* God." This drove such a wedge between them that now the very mention of Christ creates tension and hostility.

As someone openly antagonistic to the Lord, Mike doesn't see holiness as something to strive for. As the animosity in their marriage grows, it will be harder for the couple to see each other as outrageous. Liz is plagued by fears that Mike was just faking all along. She wonders: *Do I even know this man I married?*

Can you imagine yourself in such a marriage? The emotional pain would be truly heartbreaking. We know of a couple in a situation similar to Liz and Mike's who have gone so far as to choose not to have children since the husband refuses to raise them in any kind of church.

The apostle Peter speaks with compassion to women in Liz's situation. He encourages them to live in "purity and reverence," so their husbands may be won to Christ by their example (1 Peter 3:1-2). (*From Jeramy:* This actually happens—in fact, it happened with my mom and dad.)

But there's no escape clause in Scripture for "marrying the wrong person." In God's eyes, the marriage vows really do apply "'til death do us part." Liz can't leave her husband, but she can pray that his heart will soften as he watches her example.

Just think how different things are for Emily. She put the brakes on her slippery slide into compromise and now has a chance to find someone H.O.T. to spend the rest of her life with. She has the chance to avoid the pain of marrying a man who doesn't share her faith.

You may think it's not all that bad to settle for a date with someone who's not really H.O.T. But once you start down the path of compromise, it's tough to turn back. You slip slowly but steadily. One day, you may find yourself engaged or married to someone whom you know isn't totally H.O.T.

We told you Aaron's story before relating Emily and Liz's experiences because we wanted to encourage you that there *are* single adults who resist the temptation to settle. Aaron knows that by refusing to settle, he honors not just the Lord, but himself as well. He realizes that waiting for the right woman will please God and make his own life better. He hasn't found that someone yet, but as he waits, he's not going to compromise.

Aim High

To keep your standards high, aim for the best at all times. As a wise man once said, "Not failure, but low aim, is crime."

Aiming high doesn't mean you date only the best looking or best dressed or the best built. That's pickiness—focusing on things that are unessential or unimportant.

The "best" we're referring to is God's best—someone who exhibits the traits that He considers essential. Throughout this book we discussed what Scripture reveals those characteristics to be. Remaining faithful to these standards is the right way to aim high and to be selective rather than picky.

Someone who's picky instead of selective might turn down a date because the person doesn't have a nice enough car, high enough career ambitions, or enough money. Pickiness looks at the surface instead of digging deep.

Selectiveness, on the other hand, looks at what really matters. A selective person looks at whether someone has walked faithfully with the Lord and shown a pattern of growth in his or her relationship with Him. Someone who is selective observes another person's personality as it's revealed in different situations. A selective person looks for someone's integrity and reliability. Someone who's selective doesn't settle in any areas because he or she knows that once you begin to give in, the force of compromise takes over.

Selective people operate on the 100 percent factor, while others settle for less. Their standards take the downward spiral that Chuck Swindoll writes about: "Excellence gets reduced to acceptable, and before long, acceptable doesn't seem worth the sweat if you can get by with adequate. After that, mediocrity is just a breath away."[1]

Once you begin to compromise your 100 percent standard, it's a short walk to mediocrity. No one ever dreams of having a mediocre relationship or marriage. Yet so many settle for that very thing.

Now the 100 percent factor doesn't mean you wait around for someone perfect. You'd be waiting a long time. Like forever.

But keep your aim at 100 percent. If you do, you're going to find someone who's aiming just as high. So aim high, targeting someone who's earnestly pursuing the things of God. Remember, if you aim at 75 percent or 50 percent or 25 percent, you're unlikely to find someone who's H.O.T.

Both of us aimed high, and we know we found someone worth finding. Yet we also went into marriage fully aware that we weren't perfect. We knew we'd have trouble and would have to let God smooth out our rough edges. But we didn't settle for mediocre or "pretty good."

Patience *Is* a Virtue

To maintain that high aim, you need to develop one skill that's tough, but well worth the effort: Patience.

How annoying was it when your parents used to say, "Patience is a virtue"? Maybe they pulled out that golden phrase when you were one hundredth in line for Space Mountain at Disneyland. Or when five other kids beat you to the ice cream counter. "You know," your mom would say, "patience is a virtue."

Yeah, yeah. We all know it. It's also one of the hardest virtues to develop.

But learning to wait patiently for a H.O.T. spouse is a must if you're going to avoid compromise. You may already have waited longer than you thought you would ever have to. Some good friends of ours waited until they were forty before they married. But they aren't complaining about how long they waited. They're one of the happiest couples we've ever seen because they know they found someone worth the wait.

Maybe you feel you can patiently wait for someone to marry, but what about someone to date? Are you anxious about who's going to ask you to the next dance or banquet? Do you sit around on Thursday night lamenting that you have no date for the weekend? Can you wait patiently for a month to find the right person to date? A year? Several years?

Hmmm....Patience seems a bit tougher when you break it down like that. Yet God calls us to be strong in patience, no matter what the situation or how long the wait.

The book of Psalms is full of admonitions to wait patiently, such as this one: "Wait for the LORD and keep his way" (37:34). The writer of Psalm 130 was someone who knew how to wait: "I wait for the LORD, my soul waits, and in his word I put my hope.... Put your hope in the LORD, for with the LORD is unfailing love and with him is full redemption." (130:5,7)

"The LORD" is the key to waiting in both these passages. As we wait for God to move, we must trust His perfect timing and His perfect will. Meanwhile His Word nourishes us during our times of waiting. And we know that ultimately God's love never fails. Serving the true Lord, we can wait patiently. The Author of our destiny has our best in mind.

If waiting makes you feel like you're doing nothing, take heart: Waiting patiently involves a lot. Patience doesn't imply sitting around and twiddling your thumbs. While you exercise patience, you can grow in a number of areas.

First, patience increases contentment. In her article, "God's Sheep Dogs," Elisabeth Elliot describes patience as a willingness to accept calmly what we have or don't have. Such calm acceptance is synonymous with contentment. Contentment allows you to get on with your life because, instead of pining after what you don't have, you're satisfied. You need not worry because whatever you have is enough.

Second, patience helps you face your own limitations. Jan Frank describes it this way in *A Graceful Waiting*, "We can't make things happen even when we try our hardest. The longer we wait, the more aware we are of our own powerlessness."[2]

We can't force dating or marriage to happen. Relationships take their own course and have their own energy, and the more we try to manipulate them, the more we find ourselves lost and helpless. We have only one option, and that is to turn our desires and dreams over to the Lord who alone can change things. We prayerfully tell the Lord our hopes, knowing that we cannot make things happen on our own. We are limited; He is not. Patience helps us to recognize this truth.

Finally, patience helps you clarify and refine your desires. "In fact," writes David Runcorn, "it helps us to recognize where our real desires lie. It separates our passing enthusiasm from our true longings. It reveals to us both our shallowness and our depths."[3]

The longer you wait to date or get married, the better idea you'll have of what you want. As you wait, the Lord can refine and shape your desires so that you focus on what is significant rather than on nonessentials.

This idea of waiting may seem strange or absurd to you. "All it would do is make me more desperate," you may plead. But from experience we can tell you that waiting does improve your vision and can help you resist the temptation to compromise. The longer you wait, the less willing you are to settle. After all, if you've made it this far, why give up now?

As you develop patience in relationships with the opposite sex, you will cultivate it in other areas of life as well. You'll be able to wait with peace because you know God has your best in mind. Waiting patiently benefits you in many ways.

Off Target

You may have already faced the temptation to compromise in a dating relationship. You may have dropped your standard and found how disappointing it can be to date someone who's not God's best. You know how hard it is to resist going out with someone you're intrigued by but who doesn't share your values.

Whether or not you've faced such a situation, these words from Oswald Chambers offer a valid warning: "Beware of leakage, of the dividing up of your life by the influence of friends or circumstances; beware of anything that is going to split up your oneness with Him…"[4]

You know what the Lord desires for you. You know that settling for anything less will take you away from Him in some way. Commit now to resisting the temptations that come your way. In doing this, you'll please the Lord and protect yourself.

God promises us, "No test or temptation that comes your way is beyond the course of what others have had to face. All you need to remember is that God will never let you down; he'll never let you be pushed past your limit; he'll always be there to help you come through it" (1 Corinthians 10:13, *The Message*). You aren't the first person to be tempted to date someone whom you know you shouldn't. You aren't the only one who's fallen in love with a man or woman you know you shouldn't marry. This verse tells us that other single Christians have faced such temptations and that God helped them through.

Decide now not to settle! You, like every child of God, deserve someone committed to being holy, outrageous, and trustworthy.

Define your convictions now and plan ahead of time how you can stick to them. God will never let you down or let you be pushed beyond what you can handle. He can help you either say no to the wrong date or get out of a relationship that may land you in a bad marriage. Let Him provide you with the way of escape from each temptation. And each time you take that path, it will be easier the next time to take it again.

Something Better

Despite all the good reasons for waiting, some Christians still aim low, get impatient, or refuse to resist temptation. Why is this?

We think it boils down to having a wrong perception of God. Christians settle because they believe God won't give them something better than what they can get for themselves.

What a false assumption! Our God "is able to do immeasurably more than all we ask or imagine" (Ephesians 3:20). The best we could dream of, pray for, or grab for ourselves can never match what God longs to do for us. Our human desires and efforts are immeasurably poor by comparison, as the following story illustrates.

Once upon a time, there was a little girl who adored jewelry.

She loved playing dress-up with her own fake gems. And she loved going with her parents to the mall to gaze at the real stones glittering in the shop windows.

During one such trip, they passed by a discount store, and the little girl spotted a pearl necklace in the window. The white beads seemed to glow. Next to the necklace, she noted the price tag. It read $4.99.

She received only a quarter for her weekly allowance. It would take her over five months to save for that precious necklace. Determined, she waited and carefully put each of her quarters in her piggy bank. Every time her parents went to the mall, she begged to go along so she could make sure the necklace hadn't been sold.

When she finally saved enough to pay for the necklace, her father took her back to the discount store. To her delight, the pearls were still waiting. She proudly walked into the store, emerging minutes later with a small velvet pouch. "I did it, Daddy!" she exclaimed.

That night, as her father tucked her into bed, he asked, "Honey, do you love me?"

"Of course I love you," his daughter replied.

"Do you love me enough to give me your pearl necklace?" her father questioned.

Horrified, she burst into tears. "Daddy, I love you, but I can't give you my pearl necklace." Her father leaned down, kissed her, and told her it was okay.

Each night for a week, the father and daughter had the same conversation. Each night, after her tearful reaction, her father kissed her just the same. Finally, on Sunday night, the father heard her crying sometime after he had tucked her in.

He opened the door to her bedroom and sat down on the bed. "Daddy," she sighed through tears, "I love you. You can have my pearl necklace."

She pulled the small velvet pouch from under her pillow, placing it in her father's hands. Now it was his eyes that filled with tears as he hugged her tightly. He thanked her and walked out of the room.

The next morning, when the little girl awoke, she felt something under her pillow. Almost forgetting that she'd given away her precious necklace, she reached for the velvet pouch. But her hand grasped something sturdier.

She pulled out a small blue box and placed it in her lap. Slowly she opened it and gasped with surprise. Inside was a genuine pearl necklace. On the clasp, an inscription read, "Daddy Loves You."

Sometimes we have to give up something that we cherish in order for God to bless us with the best. We may have to sacrifice going on a date to wait for someone who's truly God's best. We might have to relinquish our "right" to a relationship with someone who isn't right for us.

Unless we know and trust that God loves us, that He has our best in mind, and that He can do far better for us than we can do for ourselves, we can never give our dreams entirely to Him. We can never resist the temptation to compromise.

But we *can* know these truths about God! He *is* able to do immeasurably more than what we imagine. He can and will bless you for sacrificing and waiting patiently.

Trust in Him, and you'll never have any need to settle. Let go of your fake pearls…so that God might give you the real thing.

H.O.T. Questions for Personal Study and Group Discussion

The Intro: About That Word . . .

1. What are your top two or three reasons for reading this book?

2. What would your friends say makes a girl or guy "hot"?

3. As you can see, the H.O.T. acronym stands for "Holy," "Outrageous," and "Trustworthy." Take those three words one at a time: What thoughts come to mind with each word?

4. Do you believe the Bible is a trustworthy guide and authority for your relationships with the opposite sex? If so, why? If you aren't convinced, what issues about the Bible raise questions in your mind?

Chapter 1: Making the Choice

1. What are the most common perceptions your friends have of marriage?

2. Look carefully at Matthew 19:3-12. What evidence do you see in this passage that God wants us to take marriage very seriously?

3. What is your understanding of why God created marriage?

4. When two Christians get married, what should their attitude toward divorce be? (Some helpful scriptures to explore: Malachi 2:16; Matthew 19:3-12; 1 Corinthians 7:10-16 and 7:27.)

5. More H.O.T. passages to explore and discuss: 1 Corinthians 7:1-5; Hebrews 13:4.

Chapter 2: Holy Is Hot

1. Jesus is called "the Holy and Righteous One" in Acts 3:14. How did Jesus demonstrate holiness in the way He lived His life?

2. Look at the command in 1 Peter 1:15-16. How do you think God's holiness should be connected to your holiness?

3. What exactly has God done in order to make you holy? (Helpful scriptures to explore are Ephesians 1:3-5 and Colossians 1:21-22.)

4. According to Hebrews 12:14, what are we supposed to do in order to be holy? And what is the most important thing you can do in your life now to obey this command?

5. More H.O.T. passages to explore and discuss: Romans 15:13; 1 Peter 2:4-5; 2 Peter 3:10-14.

Chapter 3: Outrageous Is Hot

1. What makes a person outrageous?

2. What personality traits make a guy or girl attractive to you?

3. In your opinion, what does it take to have real joy in life? And what can take that joy away?

4. When you see someone of the opposite sex who is physically attractive to you, what do you think is the best way to think about that person, from God's point of view?

5. More H.O.T. passages to explore and discuss: Romans 12:1-2; Ephesians 5:8-10 and 5:15-20; 1 Thessalonians 5:16-19.

Chapter 4: Trustworthy Is Hot

1. In your opinion, why is trust an important factor in any friendship?

2. How does the lack of trust hurt a friendship?

3. How does trusting God help a person to be better able to trust other people?

4. How does trusting God help a person to be more trust-worthy?

5. Look at the words of Jesus in Luke 16:10. How does this principle apply to relationships?

6. What are the most important things you can do to be trustworthy in your relationships?

7. More H.O.T. passages to explore and discuss: Matthew 24:45-
   51; 1 Corinthians 4:2; 2 Corinthians 8:21; Colossians 3:9-10.

Chapter 5: He's H.O.T.

1. Remembering especially what you have read in this chapter,
   list what you think are the most important qualities of…

   a. a holy man.

   b. an outrageous man.

   c. a trustworthy man.

2. Look again at your answers to the above question. Then compare the qualities you listed to the kind of hot guy image that's

commonly presented in magazines, movies, and TV programs. In what ways does the world's image most differ from God's standards?

3. What do you think a young Christian man should be learning now in order to be a good husband when he gets married? (Helpful scriptures to explore: Ephesians 5:25-33; Colossians 3:19; 1 Peter 3:7.)

4. More H.O.T. passages to explore and discuss: Titus 2:6; 1 Peter 5:5.

Chapter 6: She's H.O.T.

1. Remembering especially what you have read in this chapter, list what you think are the most important qualities of...

    a. a holy woman.

    b. an outrageous woman.

    c. a trustworthy woman.

2. Look again at your answers to the above question. Then com-
    pare the qualities you listed to the kind of hot woman image
    that's commonly presented in magazines, movies, and TV pro-
    grams. In what ways does the world's image most differ from
    God's standards?

3. What do you think a young Christian woman should be
    learning now in order to be a good wife when she gets mar-
    ried? (Helpful scriptures to explore: Ephesians 5:22-24;
    Colossians 3:18; 1 Peter 3:1-6.)

4. More H.O.T. passages to explore and discuss: 1 Timothy
    2:9-10; Titus 2:3-5.

Chapter 7: How H.O.T. Are You?

1. Look at 1 Corinthians 7:32-35. What are the most important
    ways that you can please God now while you're single?

2. This chapter speaks of how God "satisfies" us. What are some ways that God actually satisfies you?

3. The Bible teaches us that prayer is the right way to respond when we feel anxious (Philippians 4:6-7) or troubled (James 5:13). Why do you think God wants us to respond this way?

4. In the last twenty-four hours, which of your thoughts and actions do you think were most pleasing to God?

5. What older, mature Christian can you meet with to help you evaluate your spiritual life?

6. More H.O.T. passages to explore and discuss: Romans 12:3; 2 Corinthians 13:5; Philippians 4:4-9; 1 Thessalonians 4:1-8; 1 Timothy 4:12.

Chapter 8: H.O.T. Talk

1. In the last week, what are the most encouraging words that someone spoke to you? How did these words help you?

2. In the last week, what are some encouraging words that you have spoken to others?

3. Look at David's prayer in Psalm 141:3. How would you express this prayer in your own words?

4. More H.O.T. passages to explore and discuss: Matthew 12:36; Ephesians 4:29-32.

Chapter 9: H.O.T. Walk

1. Look at everything we're told about the day in Brian's life. In what ways was his day similar to a typical day for you? In what

ways was it different? What did you admire most about how
Brian handled the various situations he faced that day?

2. Look at Colossians 3:23. Think of some task or responsibility
   you commonly face which you don't like doing. What does it
   mean practically for you to do it "with all your heart, as working for the Lord"?

3. Look up Proverbs 3:5-6. Practically speaking, how can you tell
   when you're depending "on your own understanding" instead
   of trusting in the Lord?

4. In 1 Timothy 5:22, Paul tells Timothy to "keep yourself pure."
   In what areas of your life do you find it most difficult to keep
   yourself pure? What can you do to keep yourself pure in God's
   eyes?

5. What are you doing regularly in your life now to grow in your understanding of the Bible?

6. More H.O.T. passages to explore and discuss: Ephesians 5:1-4; Colossians 3:12-17.

Chapter 10: H.O.T. Meets H.O.T.

1. Discuss the importance of open communication in relationships. In what ways did defining their relationship and communicating clear intentions help Alex and Kaitlyn?

2. If you were (or are) in a relationship similar at any stage to Alex and Kaitlyn's, in what ways would following their example be easiest for you? In what ways would it be more difficult?

3. What do you believe are the most important guidelines and principles for engaged couples to follow?

4. More H.O.T. passages to explore and discuss: Genesis 2:18-25; Ecclesiastes 4:9-12; 1 Corinthians 13:4-7.

Chapter 11: Real H.O.T.

1. Do you think it's wrong to date for the time being someone who doesn't measure up to your H.O.T. standards? Why or why not?

2. What are your most important convictions and standards in choosing someone to date?

3. What kind of situations, if any, would most likely cause you to compromise your dating standards and convictions? How can you prepare yourself for this danger?

4. In your life right now, what are the most important areas in which God wants you to be patient and to wait for His timing?

5. Think about the story of the little girl and the fake pearls. In what ways can you identify with this girl?

6. More H.O.T. passages to explore and discuss: Ephesians 3:20-21; James 5:7-8.

Notes

Chapter 1: Making the Choice

1. Dennis and Barbara Rainey, *Moments Together for Couples* (Ventura, Calif.: Regal Books, 1995), January 13–15.

Chapter 2: Holy Is Hot

1. A. W. Tozer, *The Pursuit of God* (Camp Hill, Pa.: Christian Publications, Inc., 1982), 106.
2. Oswald Chambers, *My Utmost for His Highest* (Westwood, N.J.: Barbour and Company, 1963), 180.
3. Jerry Bridges, *The Pursuit of Holiness* (Colorado Springs: NavPress, 1978), 14.
4. Tozer, *Pursuit of God*, 7.
5. J. I. Packer, *Knowing God* (Downers Grove, Ill.: InterVarsity Press, 1973), 32.
6. Eugene Peterson, *A Long Obedience in the Same Direction* (Downers Grove, Ill.: InterVarsity Press, 1980), 12.

Chapter 3: Outrageous Is Hot

1. Peterson, *Long Obedience*, 92.

Chapter 4: Trustworthy Is Hot

1. Shakespeare, *Henry V,* act 2, scene 3, line 53.
2. Roy Hession, *The Calvary Road* (Fort Washington, Pa.: Christian Literature Crusade, 1950), 55-6.
3. Chambers, *My Utmost,* 211.

Chapter 6: She's H.O.T.

1. Ruth Stafford Peale, "A Few Kind Words for Femininity," in *For Women Only,* ed. Evelyn R. and J. Allan Petersen (Wheaton, Ill.: Living Books, 1974), 76.
2. Cynthia and Robert Hicks, *The Feminine Journey* (Colorado Springs: NavPress, 1994), 55.
3. Quoted by Peale, *For Women Only,* 20.

Chapter 8: H.O.T. Talk

1. John Powell, *Why Am I Afraid to Tell You Who I Am?* (London: Fontana, 1975).

Chapter 9: H.O.T. Walk

1. Richard Foster, *Celebration of Discipline* (San Francisco: HarperCollins Publishers, 1988), 130.
2. Chambers, *My Utmost,* 42.
3. Foster, *Discipline,* 33.
4. Chambers, *My Utmost,* 180.
5. Jerry Bridges, *The Practice of Godliness* (Colorado Springs: NavPress, 1983), 44.

6. Charles R. Swindoll, *The Tale of the Tardy Oxcart* (Nashville, Tenn.: Word Publishing, 1998), 370.

Chapter 10: H. O. T. Meets H. O. T.
1. Chambers, *My Utmost,* 270.

Chapter 11: Real H. O. T.
1. Swindoll, *Tardy Oxcart,* 372.
2. Jan Frank, *A Graceful Waiting* (Ann Arbor, Mich.: Vine Books, 1996), 117.
3. David Runcorn, *A Center of Quiet: Hearing God When Life Is Noisy* (Downer's Grove, Ill.: InterVarsity Press, 1990), 88.
4. Chambers, *My Utmost,* 170.

Acknowledgments

To our Lord and Savior:

Your gracious blessing has touched every part of our lives. Thank you for this fairy-tale adventure of being authors. Thank you for redeeming the mistakes and failures of our past relationships. Thank you for the gift you have given us in each other and in the covenant of marriage. Thank you for loving us first. Thank you for dying that we might live. We love you, and we exalt you!

To those whose hands have molded this work:

Thomas Womack, the "king" of editing. With wisdom, skill, and willingness, you transformed this project. Yet we cherish your friendship even more than your professional expertise. Thank you for dialoguing with us, supporting our ministry, and loving us like family.

Doug Gabbert, the "idea man." Your extreme passion for life and your consistent challenge to take things beyond the limits have stretched us. Thank you for standing by us for two years and two books.

LeAnn Redford, the "shark." Thank you for not turning our book into a pamphlet. You offered such profound insight and direction. You refused to let us get away with the mediocre (or the safe). Thank you.

Louie and Louise Moesta, thanks for riding with us on this Mexican train! Your candid dissection of our manuscript gave this book grammatical, structural, and most importantly, scriptural integrity. We adore you both.

Brian Aaby, who has been sounding board, editor, partner. God has blessed you with ideas, experience, and the unique ability to rejoice with those that are rejoicing.

Jen Wilson, a truly H.O.T. young woman. We can't wait to see what God has in store for you.

To our family:

Mom and Dad Clark, we long to be nearer. Your loving prayers have "put a hedge around us." Mom, your laughter echoes in our hearts. Your joy is infectious and Christlike. Dad, your sound wisdom has guided us time and again. We admire your strength and godly leadership.

Mom and Dad Redford, we pray the Lord will allow us to live closer. Nothing compares to your generous and gracious love. Mom, you are a confidante and cheerleader. You are a woman of truth and discernment. Dad, we delight in your creativity, intensity, and passion. Thank you for being like the Son of Laughter, a man who wrestles in faith.

Ian Redford, we've enjoyed watching you grow in the Lord. We have fond memories of your involvement in our dating and engagement.

Jonathan Redford, the Lord has blessed you with so many talents. We know your stability and strong leadership will continue to influence lives for Christ.

Jessica and John Hoelle, we admire your wholehearted devotion to each other. Your love is more precious than Mulder and Scully's ever could be.

Dave, Denise, Chase, and Emilee Clark, we praise God for your renewed zeal and desire to honor God as a family. We wish we could float down more rivers together.

Nan and Art, we've enjoyed our double dates! Thank you for investing in our marriage.

To the friends whose lives have impacted ours:

"The Crew." Brian Aaby, Anthony Naimo, and Darryl Goltiao. Our friendship is unparalleled. Your continual sharpening, encouragement, and accountability bring life and joy.

Adam and Katie Dorband, your story is one worth writing about. May our friendship continue to grow, and may God glorify Himself in your marriage and ministry.

Carl and Marcia Lachman, you know who you are, and now others do too! Our times together are too few and far between. We respect you, and we look forward to a lifelong friendship.

The TLC team. Adam Dorband and Clint Rosebush. It's a thrill to minister alongside young men of your caliber. Your fire for God and excitement for His work are contagious.

If you would like to contact
Jeramy and Jerusha Clark,
please write to them at:
igavedatingachance@hotmail.com